21st Century Ceramics

in the United States and Canada

Related Titles by The American Ceramic Society

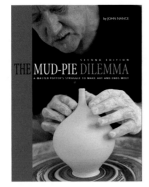

The Mud-Pie Dilemma by John Nance

For more than three decades, studio potters Tom and Elaine Coleman have sustained themselves and raised a family through their work in clay. It has involved major changes in geography, and in ways, styles and means of living and working. Despite the difficulties and occasional setbacks, the Colemans have found it to be a personally and creatively gratifying career.
Author John Nance, who met the Colemans 25 years ago when he documented their work in the first edition, brings their story up to date in this latest edition.

Rudio Autio by Louana M. Lackey

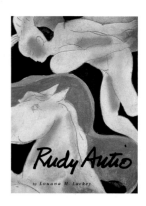

Rudio Autio is considered one of the most important and influential ceramics artists working in the United States in the last fifty years. With works in permanent collections of museums around the world including the Museum of Arts and Design, the Boston Museum of Fine Arts, the Metropolitan Museum of Art, the Renwick Gallery, and the Aichi and Shigaraki ceramic museums in Japan, Rudy Autio has left an indelible mark on the world with his art. This exciting book celebrates Autio's life and work, and features a stunning gallery of more than 150 color images.

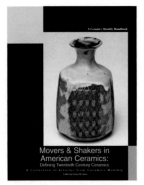

Movers & Shakers in American Ceramics:
Defining Twentieth Century Ceramics by Elaine Levin

This remarkable collection of *Ceramics Monthly* articles, written by Elaine Levin over a period of 25 years, tells the story of some of the most notable figures of the ceramic art movement in the United States during the 20th century.
Levin relates the often long struggles and ultimate successes of 26 Movers and Shakers who dedicated their lives to a single vision- unselfishly pushing ceramic art into uncharted territory so others could enjoy and benefit from their efforts. From Binns, Baggs, Robineau and the Windenhains, through Voulkos and Soldner, to Saxe, Rothman and Olsen, these personal stories are sure to educate and inspire ceramics artists well into the 21st century.

Wood Firing: Journeys and Techniques Foreword by Dick Lehman

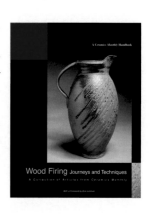

For some potters, wood is more than just a source of fuel for a kiln, it is a process. Wood firing can provide a link for ceramics artist to their surroundings and to pottery's beginnings thousands of years ago. Here are the experiences of potters who have sought to reconnect with a basic technology and who want to explore and master all the possible variables that this technique provides for the creative process. This book describes some of the technical, safety and physical challenges of wood firing through first-hand accounts and interviews with potters.

21st Century Ceramics

in the United States and Canada

Bill Hunt, *editor & curator*

Natalie R. Marsh, *copy editor & director of exhibitions*

Mindy Good, *curatorial & production assistant*

Published in conjunction with the exhibition,
21st Century Ceramics in the United States and Canada,
presented October 10 through December 7, 2003
at the Columbus College of Art & Design,
Columbus, Ohio, U.S.A.

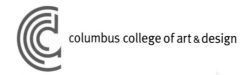

columbus college of art & design

Contents

ON THE COVER: "Skill and Reason," 18 inches (46 cm) in height, thrown, glazed earthenware with wire mesh and metal wall pedestal, by John Goodheart, Bloomington, Indiana, photo: Kevin Montague, Michael Cavangh

ON THE BACK COVER: "Commemorative Dish for 21st Century Ceramics: Pottery," 18 inches (46 cm) in width, thrown earthenware, decoration in the style of 17th-century English slipware, by Irma Starr, Kansas City, Missouri.

Acknowledgements

This project received the most extensive and creative kinds of support from the administration, faculty and staff of the Columbus College of Art & Design (CCAD). Its forward-looking administration, under the presidency of Denny Griffith, has created a culture of possibility and opportunity for everyone at the college. This underlying attitude pervaded every aspect of our project: to create a blockbuster ceramics exhibition and a book based on it.

Provost Anedith Nash supported the project as an important part of the college's educational mission, and this was no small commitment for an art college. This project involves the largest and most complex exhibition in its history.

Murley Miller, Stephanie Hightower, Pam Bishop, Tracey Moran and Elizabeth Stackpole in the Development Office worked endless hours to help fund and promote it. They gained important corporate support and grants from the Ohio Arts Council and the Greater Columbus Arts Council.

Jennifer McNally, Lacey Luce, Mark Johnson and Michael Lai in CCAD's Communications Department were highly successful in a maximum effort to promote it through magazines, newspapers, radio and television. Tom Green and Brooke Hunter-Lombardi in Admissions shared and mailed a poster for the project (designed by Stephanie Maruschak) when it needed an extra push in advertising, and helped promote it to the region's secondary-school students.

Before and during the event, Char Norman of Continuing Education and Nanette Hayakawa of Fine Arts helped with the myriad details of organizing workshops with Val Cushing, Josh DeWeese, Mary Roehm and Bobby Silverman.

Natalie R. Marsh, Christopher Yates, Tamara Peterson, Mindy Good and Brent Payne performed in quality and quantity beyond belief by handling the stacks of paperwork, hours of editing, dozens of phone calls, days of scanning, acres of boxes, unpacking, mounting, repacking art, layout and design, production, writing and hundreds of details, details, details. Natalie Marsh, director of exhibitions at CCAD has been a guiding light, a calm, professional and thoughtful voice in the face of impending deadlines, organizational needs and the vast workload involved in making all this happen. She labored tirelessly, often seven days a week, while wearing so many hats it's hard to count them all: curator, editor, contact person, writer, manager, cheerleader, psychologist and many more.

Bruce Robbins of Information Technology saved us from one technical problem to another.

Curt Benzle and Kaname Takada of Dimensional Studies gave many kinds of support, time, hard work and encouragement.

I expect many volunteers to sign up to help with the massive task of unpacking, mounting and repacking the exhibition, but their names cannot be recorded here because at this writing, works have not yet arrived for exhibition.

Then there were the artists themselves, many of whom made special pieces for the show, hand-delivered works too large or fragile for shipping and significant ceramist/authors listed on the previous contents page gave us their writing to use in this book. Ceramists Linda Arbuckle, Curt Benzle, Richard Burkett, Peter Callas, Robin Hopper, Dick Lehman, Susan Peterson and Neil Tetkowski along with dealer Andrea Fisher helped with both suggestions for artists to include and with addresses or other contact information to help make invitations possible.

Irma Starr, president of the Art Division at the American Ceramic Society, gave an impassioned plea to Glenn Harvey, Executive Director at the Society, in favor of the book while Tim Frederich, and Derek Gordon added their voices to Irma's. Mark Mechlenborg and Bill Jones approved and polished the numbers to make this book a reality. John Wilson kept production on schedule.

My wife, Liz Hunt, gave so much support, time and talent to this curator/editor, even while she was preparing for an exhibition of her own. She is a wonderful partner whom I love, respect and admire.

And finally, it's significant to note that not a person listed in these acknowledgements benefited financially from this project except earning their day-to-day salary, which they would have received anyway.

So to all who have the opportunity to look inside these pages, thank you and enjoy. We all did this for you. — B.H.

Preface

This book is the culmination of many years of planning and one idea: that there should be, at the beginning of this millennium, a significant record of the accomplishments of top ceramists. This would serve as a touchstone from which collectors, artists and scholars could look backward and forward to help understand a major phenomenon in the worlds of art and design. That phenomenon is the contemporary ceramics movement in all its diversity. Never before has there been so much quality with such breadth of thought and work. And never before have there been so many people actively making ceramics worldwide.

Out of this extensive interest has come a marvelous body of work, some of the best of which are shown within these pages. Any listing of important ceramists that represents only 250 of them, without question leaves out many fine people. Given enough funding and stamina, this book or its underlying exhibition could easily have shown a top 1000 without any loss of quality. Some important ceramists not shown here were unavailable during the organizational phase of this project; others were working internationally in places that made shipping impossible. Consequently, those left out of this documentation remain in good company.

The success of such a large-scale project was considered by many good people to be impossible, particularly in a year of reduced funding for the arts. Both the exhibition and the book really weren't supposed to happen. Nevertheless, through tireless work, and belief and tenacity exhibited by many people around the continent, but particularly at Columbus College of Art & Design, "21st Century Ceramics in the United States and Canada," opened October 10, 2003 at the colllege's 10,000-square-foot Canzani Center Gallery in Columbus, Ohio. As guest curator of this show, I wanted to cure three ills I had encountered over a long career in ceramics. The first is the problem of curators who don't fully understand ceramics, nevertheless selecting such work, often for important exhibitions. The second

is that ceramics shows are usually presented on a small scale, unlike the blockbuster exhibitions often associated with the works of famous painters and sculptors. And third is the problem of how to make the influence of the exhibition last long after the show ends.

The second problem was easy to fix. Invite 250 of the best ceramists, potters, ceramic sculptors (or whatever you like to call them) within the United States and Canada. I had been collecting addresses since 1994 when I left my former career as the editor of *Ceramics Monthly* magazine. And I knew many people who were knowledgeable in regions of the continent where I was not. So a list could be put together and contact made with the artists.

The first problem was more difficult: How to bring the artist's expertise into the curatorial equation? The answer was to ask the artists to select their own best work for the show. They know their intent better than anyone, they know how successful a piece is and can vouch for its technical excellence.

The third problem was solved through the generosity of the American Ceramic Society, which agreed to publish, instead of a typical catalog, this book that would last for years to come. And one of the principle reasons for this intended longevity is a selection of significant essays by some of the best minds in the field. Of course, they don't agree, but they do frame the thinking from within the so-called field of ceramics at the current time.

The resulting document in your hand was thus engineered out of respect for the artists, yet, without compromise, it should serve the interests of all who look inside. I hope you find something to love and something to challenge your aesthetic standards here, as well as something to make you think and to change you in a positive way. For in the end, the purpose of this art is its impact, whether on the viewer, the user or the maker.

— Bill Hunt

"Slots", 28 inches (71 cm) in height, wood-fired stoneware, photo: Dean Adams

"Holes," 28 inches (71 cm) in height, wood-fired stoneware, photo: Dean Adams

Richard Aerni

Bloomfield, New York

Photo: Maisne Dickman

"Gondola Tray," 12 inches (30 cm) in width, thrown and altered stoneware, once fired with ash glazes

Bowl, 20 inches (51 cm) in diameter, thrown stoneware with slips, multiple ash glazes, single fired to Cone 10

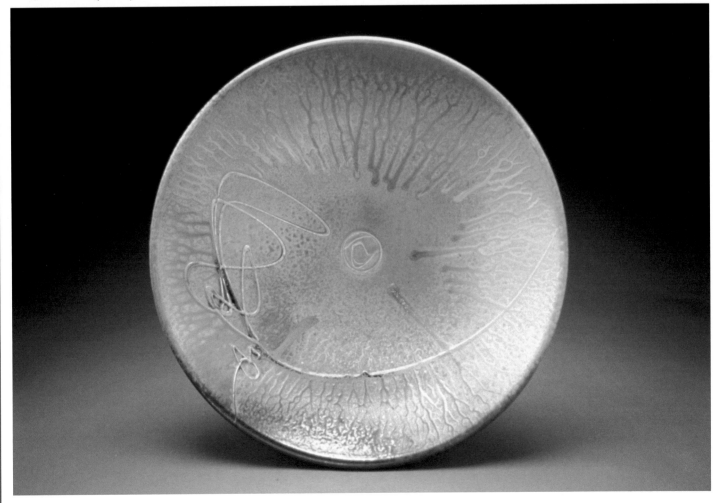

Stanley Mace Andersen

Bakersville, North Carolina

Tureen and Plate, 12 inches (30 cm) in height, thrown and altered earthenware, majolica glaze under stain brushwork, fired to Cone 03 in oxidation

Photos: Tom Mills

Coffee Server, 10.25 inches (26 cm) in height, thrown and altered earthenware with majolica glaze under stain brushwork, fired to Cone 03 in oxidation

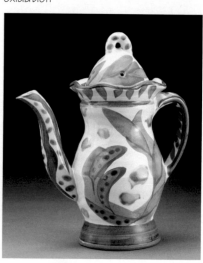

Dan Anderson

Edwardsville, Illinois

"Shell Water Tower," 12.5 inches (32 cm) in height, wheel-thrown stoneware, wood fired with low-fire decal, sandblasted, photo: Jeffery Bruce

"Gulf Water Tower," 10.75 inches (27 cm) in height, wheel-thrown stoneware, wood fired with low-fire decal, sandblasted, photo: Jeffery Bruce

Frederica Antonio

Acoma, New Mexico

Vessel, handbuilt earthenware
with slip decoration

Vessel, handbuilt earthenware
with slip decoration

Photo: Randy Batista

Linda Arbuckle

Micanopy, Florida

"Square Bowl: Twos on Red," 8.25 inches (21 cm) in height, majolica on terracotta, thrown and altered, photo: Linda Arbuckle

"Oval: Toward Fall," 4.5 inches (11 cm) in height, majolica on terracotta, photo: Linda Arbuckle

Adrian Arleo

Lolo, Montana

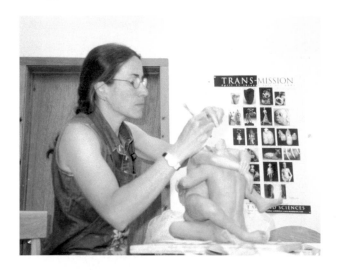

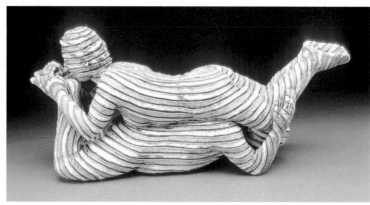

"Land & Sky," 9 inches (23 cm) in height, glazed low-fire clay, photo: Chris Autio

"Woman with Reclined Blue Child," 11 inches (28 cm) in height, glazed low-fire clay with gold luster, photo: Chris Autio

"Memorial," 34 inches (86 cm) in height, handbuilt and salt-glazed stoneware with underglazes, photo: David Emitt Adams

"Urn for the Unconceived," 24 inches (61 cm) in height, stoneware with gold leaf, cork, stamped and sprigged markings, photo: www.claytonbailey.com

Max Nanao

Doug Baldwin

Missoula, Montana

"Large Tray with Ducks," 3 inches (8 cm) in height, terracotta

"Small Ball Game," 4 inches (10 cm) in height, terracotta with white underglaze

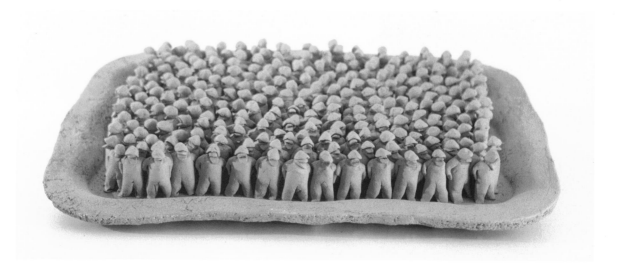

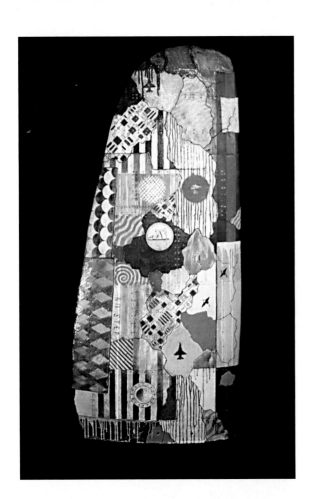

"Wing-Map," 81 inches (206 cm) in height, salt-fired stoneware with slips and glaze, photo: David Emitt Adams

"Jet," 24 inches (61 cm) in height, salt-fired stoneware, photo: David Emitt Adams

Platter With Handhold, 20 inches (51 cm) in width, stoneware, handbuilt with multiple slips and glaze, photo: Wayne Fleming

Basin With Ears, 18.5 inches (47 cm) in width, stoneware, handbuilt with multiple slips and glazes, photo: Wayne Fleming

"Pair on Base Master #1000," 7.5 inches (19 cm) in height, pit fired, painted, gilded earthenware

"Triple on Base Master #803," 18.5 inches (47 cm) in height, pit fired, painted, gilded earthenware

Carrier, 5 inches (13 cm) in height, thrown, high-fire reduced stoneware, porcelain cups, photo: Harrison Evans

Ewer, 12 inches (30 cm) in height, high-fire reduced porcelain, photo: Harrison Evans

Susan Beiner

Redlands, California

"Hidden Agenda: Hair-Do #2," 14 inches (36 cm) in height, handbuilt and slip-cast porcelain, soda fired to Cone 10

"New Hybrids," each 6 inches (15 cm) in height, slip-cast and assembled porcelain, Cone 6 gas fired

Joe Bennion

Spring City, Utah

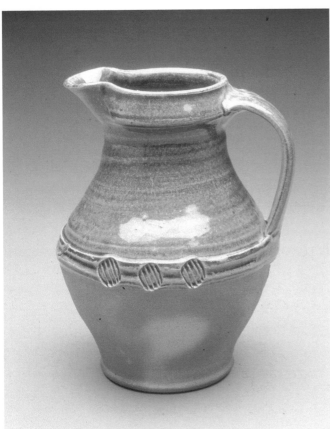

Faceted Tea Bowl, 4.5 inches (11 cm) in height, salt-glazed stoneware, photo: Richard Stum

Pitcher, 7.5 inches (19 cm) in height, thrown and wood-fired stoneware, photo: Richard Stum

Photo: Mark Anderson

Curtis Benzle

Hilliard, Ohio

"Life Flutters By," 7 inches (18 cm) in height, colored and handbuilt vitreous porcelain, gold leaf base, photo: Curt Benzle

"Break on Through," 8 inches (20 cm) in height, vitreous colored porcelain, gold leaf base, photo: Curt Benzle

Rick Berman

Atlanta, Georgia

"Salku Vase," 9 inches (23 cm) in height, thrown salku fired to Cone 10, photo: Bart Kasten

"Salku Bottle," 9.5 inches (24 cm) in height, thrown, salku (salt and raku) fired to Cone 10, photo: Bart Kasten

Luis Bermudez

Los Angeles, California

Photos: Anthony Cunha

"El Caracol," 16 inches (41 cm) in height, castable refractory with barium texture glaze and glazed earthenware

"Las tre Culebras," 13 inches (33 cm) in height, Castable refractory with barium texture glaze

"Swan," 28 inches (71 cm) in height, multifired terracotta and found objects, photo: William Triesch Voelker

Mary Jo Bole

Columbus, Ohio

"Granny's Necklace (A Bench)," 16 inches (41 cm) in height, mosaic in silicon grout with bronze, photo: Chas Ray Krider

"Plaque," 14 inches (36 cm) in height, mosaic chips on refractory material, photo: Chas Ray Krider

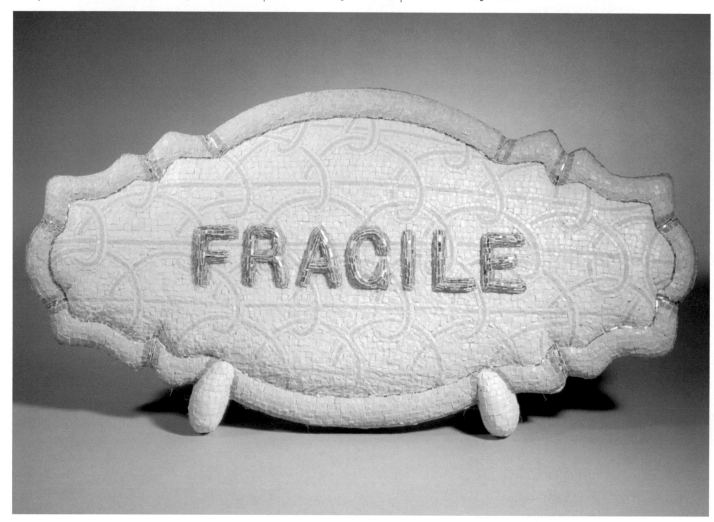

Joe Bova

Guysville, Ohio

"Red Monkey Jar," 14 inches (36 cm) in height, glazed and salt-fired porcelain

"Rabbit Canopic," 13 inches (33 cm) in height, glazed and salt-fired porcelain

"2 Owl vase," 11.5 inches (29 cm) in height, wood-fired porcelain, photo: Anne Rybak

"Speaking with Herons," 11.5 inches (29 cm) in height, wood-fired porcelain, photo: Anne Rybak

Bruce Breckenridge

Madison, Wisconsin

"Huntington Park #18," 57.75 inches (147 cm) in width, digitally glazed ceramic tiles

"Huntington Park #19," 53.75 inches (137 cm) in width, digitally glazed ceramic tiles

Photos: Greg Anderson Photography

Richard Bresnahan

Collegeville, Minnesota

Jar, 19.5 inches (50 cm) in height, coiled and paddled local stoneware, natural ash glaze, wood fired, Johanna kiln's front firemouth chamber, photo: Gary Mortenson

Teapot (with reed Krueger handle), 6.5 inches (17 cm) in height, wood fired, Johanna kiln, Tanegashima chamber, photo: Gary Mortenson

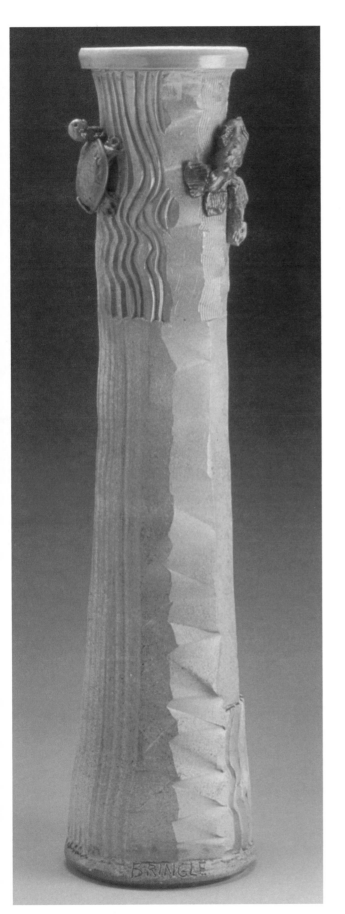

Set of 6 Goblets, thrown porcelain, salt and soda fired, photo: Tom Mills

"Vessel with Turtle & Fish," 28 inches (71 cm) in height, thrown and faceted stoneware, wood fired with salt, photo: Tom Mills

The Relevance of Hand-Made Pottery

in the Twenty-First Century

Harvey Sadow

In this high-tech world, what is the relevance of the hand-made pot? I once heard it said that there are two kinds of people: those who think that there are two kinds of people and those who don't. So before I start discussing "two kinds of pottery," please understand that I don't necessarily think that it's as black and white as all that. But lets say for the purpose at hand that there are pots designed to perform a function (for example, tableware), and those whose primary functions are purely visual and/or communicative. Yes, of course there are works which cross those lines, and no, I don't think that there are just two kinds of people either!

Let's talk tableware first. What's the relevance of the hand-made pot in our increasingly plastic world? After all, we have Tupperware, Corningware, dishes that bounce when you drop them, cups that float and millions of commercial dinnerware patterns produced by thousands of factories around the world. Even architects are designing dinnerware these days. Decals of cartoon characters and corporate logos glare back at you as you raise your cup to your lips.

I do not primarily make functional pottery. Instead, I search for and have found studio pottery so rich and beautiful, so unpretentious that it sings in harmony with the food it contains. It is a joy to choose the pieces with which to set the table. It feels so good to touch, and it is so beautiful that I can't wait to clean my plate and reveal what is beneath the food.

Since developing an interest in hand-made pottery, I even like washing the dishes. There is anticipation in fishing around in the murky, sudsy water. Removing the grime and soap is a ritual of revelation. Quirks of potter and process delight me. The hand of the potter is revealed, as is the decision-making process. There is so much to consider: size, proportions, color, whether the piece should sit solidly on the table or balance delicately and demand extra concentration in handling. Sometimes I find that pieces become more (or less) attractive over years of handling and examination. Fear and doubt cannot be hidden in a potter's work. The pieces I like best are bold, lively and fearless. Lifting a glob of soggy earth onto the potter's wheel is a hopeful act, or it should be. Commercial china is examined for its consistency. I examine studio work for its confidence. Mikasa has some nice patterns, but that stuff is why dishwashers were invented. In my last home, the dishwasher was broken when I moved in, and still was when I sold the place.

Artists have used the pottery format since the dawn of history. Those Cycladic water vessels from the Mediterranean, decorated with flowing octopus tentacles, have stayed in my mind since my first art history class, along with those little clay fertility figures, original sculptures from the dawn of culture, seldom since matched in grace, beauty or metaphorical content. Chinese, Japanese and Korean artists throughout history have painted as expressively on their pottery as on scrolls or walls. They do not separate fine and applied arts. Art is art and everything else is everything else. In Japan, the wood kilns of Bizen and Shigaraki have, for ages, produced vessels painted by the flow of fire and ash. The resulting effects are color field abstractions in brilliant and subtle earth tones. How new were the ideas of the abstract expressionists and the color-field painters in mid-twentieth century America? Perhaps they're not so new at all.

While I agree with the criticism leveled at some contemporary ceramic artists that their ideas merely restate or paraphrase those previously expressed in other media, I am not sure that this knife doesn't cut both ways. What, after all, did they use to make those paintings in the caves of Lascaux, and on those rock walls in the Australian outback? Clay, of course! Look at the Greeks. They painted everything about their lives, Gods and heroes on clay pots with clay pigments. And what about pre-Colombian ceramics: talk about your freedom of artistic expression!

I don't really want or need to travel all the way back through history to make a case for viewing pottery as fine art. Why bother? The contemporary rhetoric about art versus craft comes down to the bottom line: the bottom line in Webster's New Collegiate Dictionary. After all the definitions of craft, and there are five of them, which I will mercifully spare you, it says, synonym: art. And after six definitions of art it says, synonym: craft. Fine art has no synonym, but it won't hurt my case to read the definitions, 1) art concerned primarily with the creation of beautiful objects. 2) an activity requiring a fine skill.

So, we are concerned, and actually have been all along, about the relevance of art in the first moments of the 21st century. For those who "live by the sword" (or the car bomb), I am not sure. For those who live by the TV, no relevance at all, I suppose, unless you perceive that entertainment is art. I won't argue that one can find art on TV, but my cable company provides us with about a million stations, and I still can't find much reason to turn it on. For most of those, who will actually open these pages and read this, the relevance is clear. Our hearts, souls and minds need nourishment. We seek new perspectives. We seek to respond to the world we live in, and to share insights and observations. Art opens doors, lets fresh air into the room, shines light into darkness, speaks about things often left unsaid. Art battles boredom. Art saves lives. Artists were born to make art.

There are extremes. One person is offended by certain subject matter, while another gags on art that exists solely to fill wall space while complimenting the sofa and the drapes. There is also just plain bad work: for instance pottery whose only value is that it separates the food from the table, but I am not interested in passing judgment on anyone else's efforts. The topic at hand is relevance.

I think that the relevance of crafts (synonym: arts) in the first moments of the 21st century is determined by the vision, convictions and actions of its makers. There are no words in our actual, defined language to distinguish art from craft based solely on the medium or the format in which one works. Painted canvas or paper has no more intrinsic value than fired clay. We are inundated with flash, glitter and a throwaway mentality designed to cheapen the life experience of people in dynamic cultures moving and changing at light-speed. Carefully conceived, well-executed, sincere statements, particularly ones that reference lasting values, are badly needed. Anything and everything that comes from and relates to a balance of body, spirit and intellect is to be welcomed, because it celebrates and honors our highest purposes and qualities as human beings. Whether we are dealing with paradox and paradigm or teapot and glaze calculation, the act of making is, in itself, pure optimism. It speaks of being here and centered today, hopeful for tomorrow, acknowledging all the makings of all the yesterdays that cumulatively led to our identities and abilities. The act of making connects us to the flint chippers of prehistory by a strong archetypal thread that runs through the caves at Lascaux, the vaults filled with terra-cotta warriors at Xian, the gardens at Giverny and the groundhog kilns of Appalachia. To take the view that whatever is currently fashionable or meets academic approval is valid, and that all else is to be dismissed with contempt is shortsighted at best and divisive at least. It serves no purpose other than to exercise conceit and prejudice, both of which are strong enough already and require no further exercise.

The flint chipper was gifted with the skills and insight to make stone into sharp tools, the cave painter was gifted to render animals onto the wall. We make pots because it is in our bones to do so. Because of that, our very existence reflects the relevance of crafts today. Just as surely, the rest of the answer exists in the well being of our audience, however small or large that may be. This leaves us with one additional consideration. We have a responsibility to ourselves and to others. We must continue to grow, to develop, to seek after skill, wisdom and understanding, and through the making that defines our vision and values, we must endeavor to acknowledge and nurture our own spirit and that of our fellow humans.

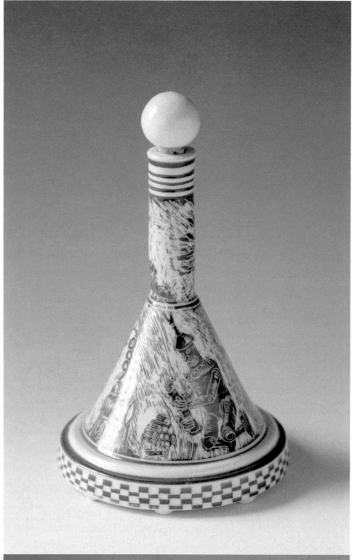

"Killer Bees: Dinnerware for Two" (detail), 12 inches (30 cm) in diameter (plate), wheel-thrown porcelain, with wax resist, glazes, fired to Cone 10 in reduction

"The Tin Man's Whiskey Bottle," two views, 10 inches (25 cm) in height, wheel-thrown porcelain, fired to Cone 10 in reduction

Barbara Brown

Sunnyvale, California

Vase Form, 10 inches (25 cm) in height, porcelain with matt black glaze, fired to Cone 10 in oxidation, photo: John Brennan

Zen Plate Series: "Earth," 12 inches (30 cm) in width, stoneware with matt black glaze, fired to Cone 10 in oxidation, photo: John Brennan

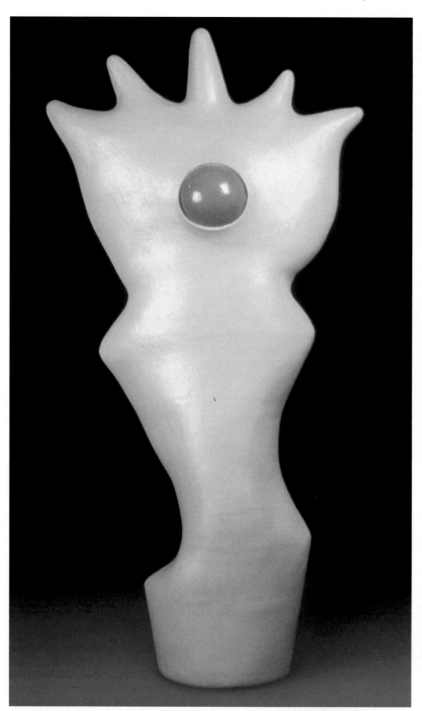

"Ra," 75 inches (191 cm) in height, slab-built ceramics, bisqued to Cone 1, with low-fire glaze

"Crown," 49 inches (124 cm) in height, slab-built ceramics, bisqued to Cone 1, with low-fire glaze

Vincent P. Burke

El Paso, Texas

"On Prufrock and other Observations #5," 5 inches (13 cm) in height, ceramics and mixed media

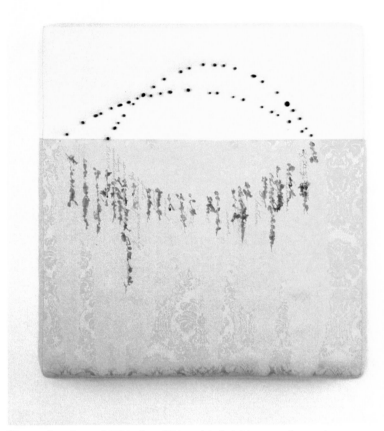

"Regarding Grace," 25 inches (64 cm) in height, ceramics and mixed media

Richard Burkett

San Diego, California

"Pressure Vessel: Overregulated," 9 inches (23 cm) in height, wheel-thrown, anagama-fired stoneware with burnout material, copper and found objects

Photo: Nan Coffin

"Pressure Vessel: Teatime for Big Oil," 8.5 inches (22 cm) in height, wheel-thrown and soda-fired porcelain with burnout material, copper and found objects

"Falling Water," 22 inches (56 cm) in height, porcelain with crystalline glaze

"Sail On," 22.5 inches (57 cm) in height, porcelain with crystalline glaze

Virginia Cartwright

Fallbrook, California

"Folded Teapot with Inlaid Cobalt
Porcelain," 7 inches (18 cm) in
height, handbuilt, unglazed exterior

Teapot Set, 6 inches (15 cm) in
height, handbuilt stoneware

Pitcher, 8 inches (20 cm) in height, thrown and wood-fired stoneware

Vase, 11 inches (28 cm) in height, thrown and wood-fired stoneware

Marek Cecula

New York, New York

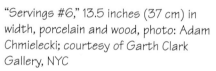

"Servings #6," 13.5 inches (37 cm) in width, porcelain and wood, photo: Adam Chmielecki; courtesy of Garth Clark Gallery, NYC

"Servings #4," 13.5 inches (37 cm) in width, porcelain and wood, photo: Adam Chmielecki; courtesy of Garth Clark Gallery, NYC

Aurore Chabot

Tucson, Arizona

"Fungus Map," 11 inches (28 cm) in height, earthenware formed by pinch construction with underglazes and stains, fired to Cone 4, photo: Balfour Walker

"Malaprop," 10 inches (25 cm) in height, earthenware formed by pinch construction with inlays, underglazes and stains, fired to Cone 4, photo: Chris Autio

Photo: Tom Storey

Paul Chaleff

Acram, New York

FAR RIGHT: Jar Form, 14 inches (36 cm) in height, wood-fired stoneware with stone inclusions

Three-Part Form, 12 inches (30 cm) in height, wood-fired stoneware with stone inclusions

Linda Christianson

Lindstrom, Minnesota

Photo: Jeff Strother

Cooking Oil Can, 9 inches (23 cm) in height, thrown stoneware, wood fired with slips and glaze, slightly salt glazed with rubber-coated wire, photo: Linda Christianson

Two Striped Plates, 1.5 inches (4 cm) in height, thrown stoneware, wood fired with slips, slightly salt glazed, photo: Linda Christianson

"Teapot (green/black)," 7 inches (18 cm) in height, slab-constructed porcelain, soda fired to Cone 10

"Teapot (black/blue dots)," 5 inches (13 cm) in height, slab-constructed porcelain, soda fired to Cone 10

A Time of Celebration for the Ceramic Arts

Phyllis Kloda

When I think about ceramics in the 21st century my mind first wanders back in history to early civilizations and then forward to the future. Ceramics has existed for humanity since the time of Cro-Magnon Man. It has been flexible and malleable in its travels over the centuries. It has withstood various periods: Classical, Renaissance, Industrialization, Bauhaus, Arts & Crafts and Post-Modernism to name a few.

As ceramists we have a common bond through time: our love for the material and our spirit of invention. We are a unique group of artists as our work evokes both our rich historical traditions and contemporary technologies. We are constantly searching for new forms, designs and surfaces that reflect the ever-changing economic and social attitudes. We are risk-takers in our way of working and undoubtedly when we subject our work to the kiln's fire. Our self-expression generates innovation and stylistic developments such as quasi-traditional forms, domestic wares, vessels, sculpture, installations and mixed media. We are no longer isolated. We connect with one another. As we zoom into the 21st century many of us are strengthening our international associations and friendships.

So, it's an exciting time to be a part of the clay community and be contributing to its history. As a community we are becoming engaged in global and multicultural arts in addition to being leaders in art technology. Among artists, some of the finest minds dealing with current science and technological issues are in ceramics. The resulting body of knowledge is a dynamic resource to move us forward with ease into the new millennium.

To our students or apprentices, who are our future, we pass on rich traditions, legacies, new insights and information to continue into the centuries ahead. We instill in them a passion for material, process, creation and diversity. We speak to them about richness of traditions and encourage them to find their own voice in clay. We challenge them to expand their visions and be self-directed in those visions. They, in turn, may pass on this legacy and sense of history to their own students.

As we move into the 21st century, this is a time of celebration of the ceramic arts. A time to contemplate both the wealth of our past and the endless possibilities of our future. A time to celebrate the growth and diversity of our community. Let the celebration begin here with the work selected for this book and exhibition!

Elaine Coleman

Henderson, Nevada

Photo: John Nance

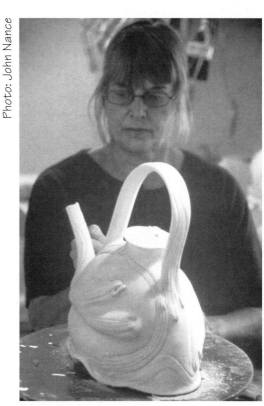

Bowl, 6 inches (15 cm) in height, porcelain, cut rim, inlaid and incised body, with white celadon glaze, photo: Tom Coleman

Covered Jar, 10.5 inches (27 cm) in height, porcelain, inlaid and incised body, with white celadon glaze, photo: Tom Coleman

Tom Coleman

Henderson, Nevada

Vase, 22 inches (56 cm) in height, thrown porcelain with various sprayed crystal matt glazes, fired to Cone 10 in reduction, photo: Tom Coleman

Photo: John Nance

White Stoneware Ikebana, 22 inches (56 cm) in length, slab-built porcelain with slips overglazed with various Shino and ash glazes, photo: Tom Coleman

Scott Cooper

Greencastle, Indiana

Fluted Celadon Vase, 11 inches (28 cm) in height, thrown porcelaineous stoneware, Cone 10 reduction, photo: Scott Cooper

Carbon Trap Shino Bowl, 2.5 inches (6 cm) in height, thrown porcelaineous stoneware, Cone 10 reduction, photo: Scott Cooper

Kevin Crowe

Amherst, Virginia

Altered vase, 14.5 inches (37 cm) in height, wheel-thrown, high-fire clay with slip surfacing, single fired over 4 days in a wood kiln, photo: Lou Saunders

Thrown and Paddled Vase, 19.5 inches (50 cm) in height, wheel-thrown, high-fire clay with slip surfacing, single fired over 4 days in a wood kiln, photo: Lou Saunders

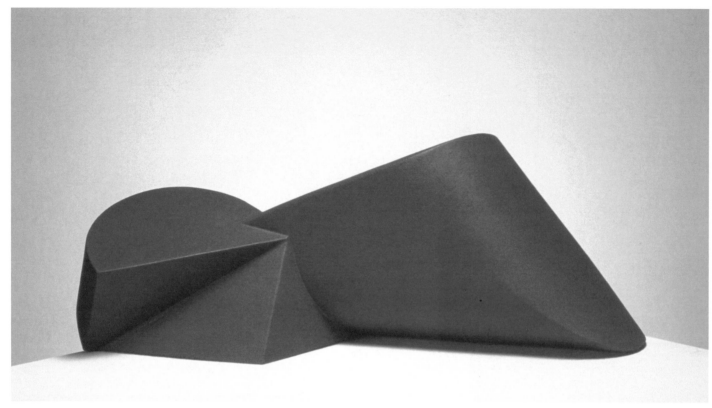

"Zoar," 23 inches (58 cm) in height, slab-constructed stoneware with low-fire glazes, photo: Brian Oglesbee

"Pivotal Moment 2002," 11 inches (28 cm) in height, slab-constructed stoneware body with low-fire glazes, photo: Brian Oglesbee

Photo: Brian Oglesbee

Val Cushing

Alfred Station, New York

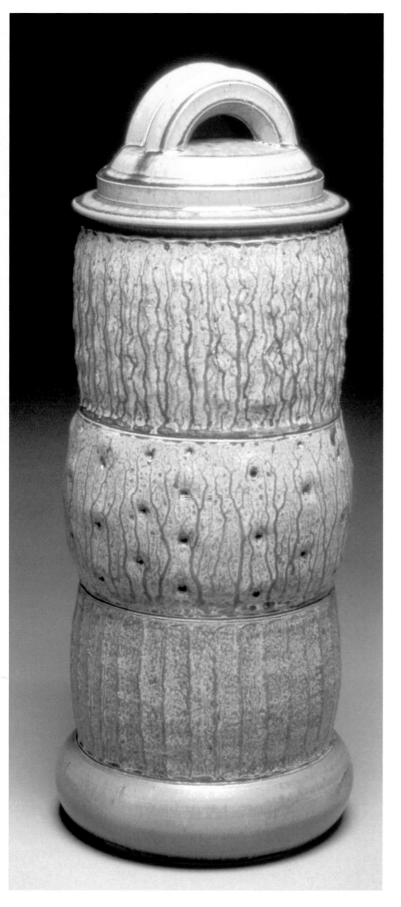

"Covered Jar/Column Series," 19 inches (48 cm) in height, thrown stoneware, fluted, high-calcium glazes, fired to Cone 9, reduction, photo: Seth Tice Lewis

"Covered Jar/Column Series," 28 inches (71 cm) in height, thrown stoneware with fluted sections, ash and satin/matt glazes, fired to Cone 9 in reduction, photo: Seth Tice Lewis

Kathy Dambach

Farmington Hills, Michigan

"Toy Series...Bobber," 56 inches (142 cm) in height, handbuilt, low-fire porcelain with vitreous slips, photo: Tim Thayer

"Toy Series...Over & Over & Over & Over," 36 inches (91 cm) in height, handbuilt, low-fire porcelain with vitreous slips, photo: Tim Thayer

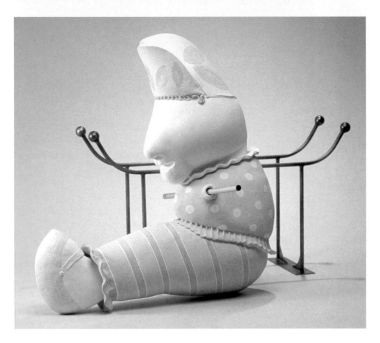

Malcom Davis

Tallmansville, West Virginia

"Personal Teapot," 6 inches (15 cm) in height, thrown porcelain with Malcolm's carbon-trap shino-type glaze

"Shino Teabowl," 3.5 inches (9 cm) in height, thrown porcelain with Malcolm's carbon-trap shino-type glaze

Harris Deller

Carbondale, Illinois

"Untitled Wall Platter with Ellipse #2,"
13 inches (33 cm) in height, handbuilt
porcelain, Cone 10 inlayed glaze,
photo: Jeff Bruce

"Untitled Wall Platter with Concentric
Arcs," 18 inches (46 cm) in height,
handbuilt porcelain, Cone 10 inlayed
glaze, photo: Jeff Bruce

Josh DeWeese

Helena, Montana

Photo: Sam Curtis

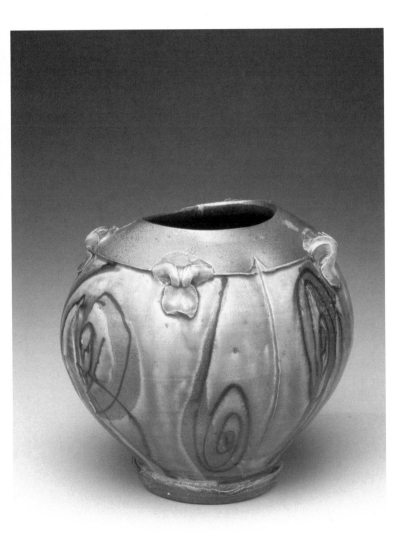

Jar, 7 inches (18 cm) in height, thrown and altered native stoneware with celadon glaze, wood-soda fired

Pitcher, 12 inches (30 cm) in height, thrown and altered stoneware with iron and copper glazes, wood-soda fired

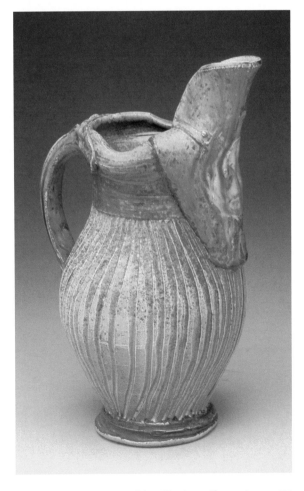

Kim Dickey

Longmont, Colorado

Photos: Nick Hudsalve

"Tart Bush," 20 inches (51 cm) in height, terracotta with glaze, on a wooden base

"Beauty Bush," 30 inches (76 cm) in height, terracotta with glaze, on a wooden base

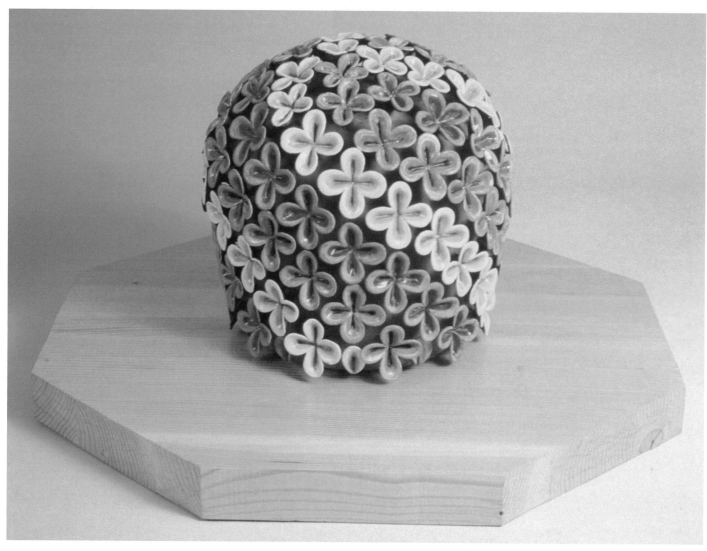

Photo: Caroline Savage

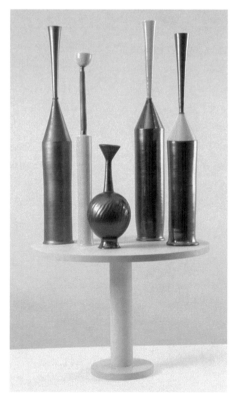

"Max and Moritz," 7 inches (18 cm) in height, thrown, low-fire clay, photo: Noel Allum

"Yellow & Black Still Life," 40 inches (102 cm) in height, thrown, low-fire clay, photo: Noel Allum

Finding a Place in the 21st Century

Bennett Bean

The beginning of the 21st century offers an opportunity never before available. We can make anything. Both historical and technical information on almost all previously produced ceramic objects is available in a cornucopia of books, images and physical examples. These are accessible to anyone as a starting point. With this many choices, the problem then becomes deciding what to make and how what we make will place us in the continuum of ceramic history. In choosing a style or the ideas we want to explore, there is no reason why this decision is not a conscious one. In doing it this way, we can also choose our niche in the ceramic subculture. The choice of the niche can either be defined through technique, the traditional way in which ceramic identity is defined, or by alignment with either a formal or ideological movement. An example of a technically-based choice would be the decision to work within the "Anagama Subculture." The qualities of this work are defined by the use of a particular kiln where the decorative decisions are deeply influenced by firing. At the other end of the spectrum is "ceramic sculpture" which offers the imagery of the art world though seldom its critical underpinnings.

To understand this, some historical explanation is appropriate. Five hundred years ago in Western culture, painting was not art. Painters were members of the guild system like the masons, gold beaters and brewers. They were patronized by the Church which hired them to illustrate teach-

ings so that the laity, who were usually illiterate, could be instructed using the painter's images. But, with the advent of the printing press and mass production of the Gutenberg Bible, the ecclesiastical work which the painters had been producing was supplanted and became mostly unnecessary. With the development of the printing press, painters had lost their socioeconomic niche. The teachings now were transmitted through the printed word. It was this event that transformed the status of painting and made it available for consideration as art. This change was not immediate but an evolving process steeped in politics and patronage.

A contemporary example of this that shows the shift from work enmeshed in the economy to work without economic viability is the evolution of the photograph. Until the 1950s we received visual information and imagery through the photograph. *Life, Look* and *Colliers* brought us photographs through which we created a sense of the world. The photographers and the magazines they supplied were literally put out of business by television. TV images replaced the still photograph as the main way by which we received visual information about the world. During the decade after the 1950s, the transformation of the photograph from photojournalism to art object can be charted by the roster of museum shows and auctions, with an attendant critical flowering legitimizing this transition. The photograph is now an accepted art form.

If the process we are enmeshed in as potter/artists is one of the emergance of ceramic-making as an art activity, what are its characteristics? Again let's refer to the history of painting. Modern painting begins with Cezanne and starts the serial exploration of the elements of traditional painting. A parallel can be drawn with diagramming a sentence. The sentence is broken into its constituent elements and the function and character of each element can be understood and analyzed separately. The Modernist painters were doing the same thing with painting — taking the elements of traditional painting and one-by-one making them the subject of their work. Picasso thought of painting as an illustration of light falling on planes and in doing so created Cubism. The Abstract Expressionists made the action of painting their central theme. In the 1960s, the last formal elements (figure/ground, depth of field and color) were isolated and explored. The final steps in this process delineated the edge of the practice of traditional painting. As typed statements appeared on gallery walls and "happenings" occurred in the streets, art-making activity moved into the realms of philosophy and theater. The edges of the activity of painting had been reached so that the role of Post-Modernism has been to reassemble these elements in new and hopefully illuminating ways.

That same thing is going on in ceramics. If you think of the historical pot in the same way painters approached traditional painting, the pot has parallel, though different, formal characteristics. Its elements included decorative surface, volume, tactility, interior space, narrative decoration, process, etc. as well as its place in ritual. There are schools representing each of these characteristics. In the case of ceramics, the same process that happened in painting is occur-

ring, though with more fits and starts than have been experienced by other media. One of the most easily recognized examples would be Peter Voulkos doing the same thing with clay that the Abstract Expressionists had done with painting.

This slow emergence of ceramics as art has been in large part because, historically, a great deal of ceramic production was utilitarian. Although much of the present ceramic production is ostensibly utilitarian, I don't believe this is its true purpose. If what the maker was actually after was utility, ceramic material would not have been selected at all because plastic, glass and metal are so much better suited for utilitarian wares. As a result, the real subject of utilitarian ceramics is the awareness of the act of use. In this way, North American utilitarian ceramics is the lineal descendent of Japanese tea ware.

The other issue that has dogged the ceramic community is the issue of "ceramic sculpture." This subgenera is especially problematic since it does result in objects that have only a superficial relationship to sculptural issues of the last century and seem much more appropriate to the conceit of the curio cabinet popular in the 1700s. Thus, ceramic sculpture often has a closer association to painting than to sculpture with its narrative content and easel-painting scale. The difficulty seems to me to be that contemporary sculpture is interested in the object as a vehicle for an idea, whereas most ceramic sculpture makes the object itself the central focus. Most of the subjects involved in ceramic sculpture borrow from the art world but lack the underpinning of art content.

"Neriage Column" (detail), 168 inches (427 cm) in height, a colored porcelain column of individual tiles from floor to ceiling

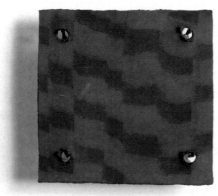

"Neriage Horizon" (detail), 120 inches (305 cm) in height, a colored porcelain horizontal linear installation of tiles

Gary DiPasquale

New York, New York

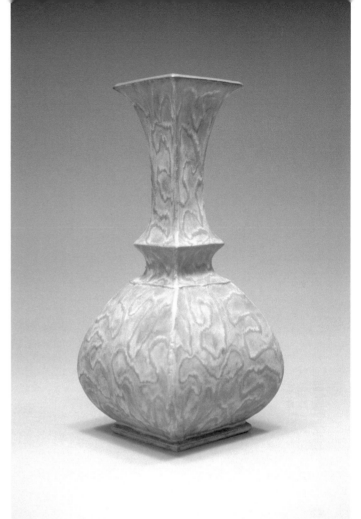

Double Neck Vase, 15.5 inches (39 cm) in height, slab-constructed stoneware with multiple glazes

Tall Vase, 24.5 inches (62 cm) in height, slab-constructed stoneware with inlayed glazes

Eddie Dominguez

Abiquiu, New Mexico

"Red Twister," 21 inches (53 cm) in height, porcelain with low-fire glazes, photo: Larry Gawell

"Road through the Storm," 21 inches (53 cm) in height, porcelain with low-fire glazes, photo: Larry Gawell

Paul Dresang

Edwardsville, Illinois

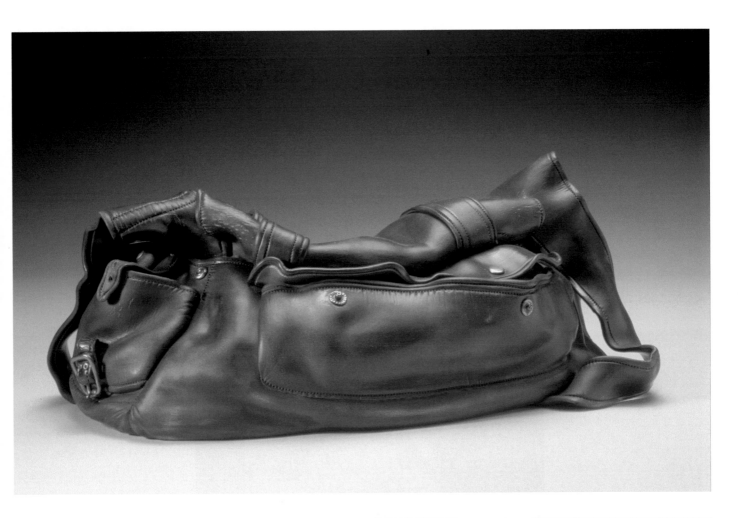

"Bag," 9 inches (23 cm) in height, thrown and slab-built porcelain, residual-salt glazed to Cone 9, with underglaze and lusters, photo: Joseph Gruber

TOP: "Photo Op," 5 inches (13 cm) in height, handbuilt porcelain, residual-salt glazed to Cone 9, with underglaze, lusters and enamels, photo: Joseph Gruber

Ed Eberle

Pittsburgh, Pennsylvania

"Black Field," 20 inches (51 cm) in height, porcelain with terra sigillata

Kim Ellington

Vale, North Carolina

Two Gallon Jar, 13.25 inches (34 cm) in height, wheel thrown with alkaline ash glaze on wood-fired local clay

Six Gallon Jar, 18.5 inches (47 cm) in height, wheel thrown with alkaline ash glaze on wood-fired local clay

Seo Eo

Greenville, North Carolina

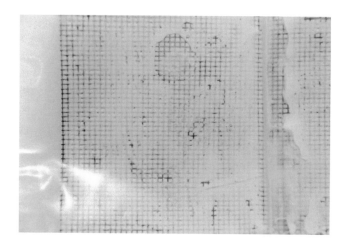

Details of "Vapor," clay, plastic, screen, salt, light; an Installation planned for the exhibition site

Paul Eshelman

Elizabeth, Illinois

"Bump Bowls," 13.5 inches (34 cm) in width, slip-cast red stoneware with glaze

"Round- and Square-Shoulder Vase," 12 inches (30 cm) in height, slip-cast red stoneware with glaze

Cary Esser

Kansas City, Missouri

"Sarracenia," 24.5 inches (62 cm) in height, press-molded and carved earthenware, terra sigillata, low-fire glaze with oxide stain, wood, photo: E. G. Schempf

"Ploughed Under," 29 inches (74 cm) in height, press-molded and carved earthenware, terra sigillata, oxide stain, wood, photo: E. G. Schempf

Christine Federighi

Coral Gables, Florida

"'Wrapped and Protected' Dog," 40 inches (102 cm) in height, oxidation-fired ceramics with oil patina

"'Wrapped and Protected' Dog Guide," 40 inches (102 cm) in height, oxidation-fired ceramics with oil patina

"White Bull On Cart," 11.5 inches (29 cm) in height, glazed porcelain bull, gold leaf horns, oak and walnut cart with brass beads and bronze wheels

"Charging Bull on Platter," 3.75 inches (10 cm) in height, black stoneware, chrome slip, Osage-orange spots

Photos: Gertrude Ferguson

Anita Fields

Stillwater, Oklahoma

"Evidence Seen," 46 inches (117 cm) in height, slab- and coil-built earthenware, surfaced with impressions from handmade stamps and incised, with underglaze

"Reaching #1," 44 inches (112 cm) in height, coil-built earthenware with terra sigillata, underglaze and gold leaf

Susan Filley

Mount Pleasant, South Carolina

Photo: Allen Rokach

"Regal Teapot - Starry Blue," 10 inches (25 cm) in height, thrown and altered porcelain, glazed, photo: Susan Filley

"Tray - Tango Twist," 14 inches (36 cm) in width, thrown and altered porcelain with glazes, photo: Susan Filley

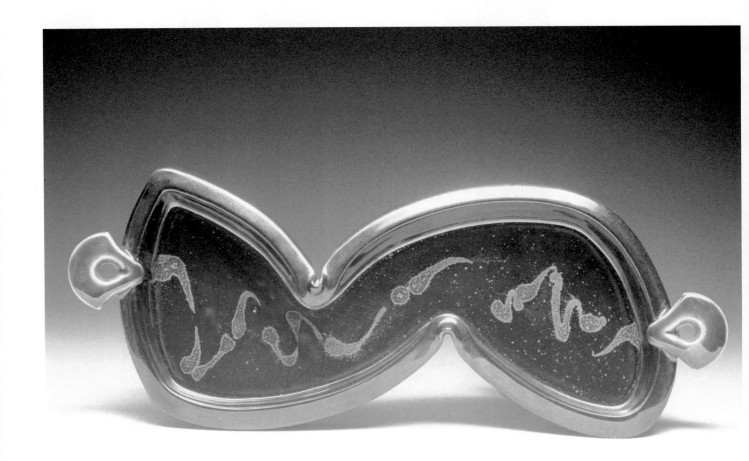

Angela Fina

Amherst, Massachusetts

Set of Five Flower Containers, the largest 16 inches (41 cm) in height, thrown porcelain, fired to Cone 11 with copper red glaze, photo: John Polak

Fan-Shaped Container for Flower Arranging, 9 inches (23 cm) in height, thrown and altered porcelain with multiple glazes fired to Cone 11, photo: John Polak

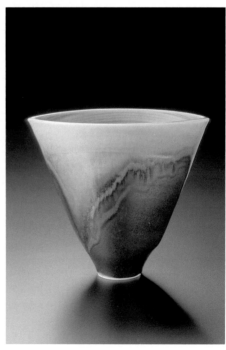

Verne Funk

San Antonio, Texas

Photo: Charlotte Funk

"Head On," 33.5 inches (85 cm) in height, slab-constructed whiteware, oil stain, fixative

"Painted Head," 34 inches (86 cm) in height, slab-constructed whiteware, oil stain, enamel

David Furman

La Verne, California

"Little Guy / Tin Can TPot," 7 inches (18 cm) in height, slip-cast midrange porcelain, underglaze, glaze, luster, enamel, photo: M. Honer

"Mama Mumbo / Tin Can TPot, 2003," 9 inches (23 cm) in height, slip-cast midrange porcelain, underglaze, glaze, luster, enamel, photo: M. Honer

John Glick

Farmington Hills, Michigan

Plate, 27 inches (69 cm) in diameter, altered stoneware with multiple slips and glazes, reduction fired to Cone 10, photo: John Glick

"Landscape View Sculpture," 10.5 inches (27 cm) in height, handbuilt stoneware, soda fired with multiple slips and glazes, fired to Cone 10, photo: John Glick

DeBorah Goletz

West Milford, New Jersey

Stacked Serving Bowls with Bud Vase, 10 inches (25 cm) in height,
thrown and altered porcelain, wood fired

Stacked Serving Set with Bud Vase, 10 inches (25 cm) in height, thrown and altered stoneware with
sprayed glaze

John Goodheart

Bloomington, Indiana

"Skill and Reason," 18 inches (46 cm) in height, thrown, glazed earthenware with wire mesh and metal wall pedestal, photo: Kevin Montague, Michael Cavangh

"End of Search," 13 inches (33 cm) in height, thrown, glazed earthenware with wire mesh and metal wall pedestal, photo: Kevin Montague, Michael Cavangh

What's the difference?

Louis Katz

We are now in the fourth year of the new century and no clear delineation has appeared to separate new art from that of the previous century. But some generalizations about ceramics over the last century can be made.

In the first part of the century the mood in clay appeared to be simple: "Clay is clay." Potters in the Western world were often associated with design schools and movements. Potters made pots. By the fifties there was a growing sense of "Clay is art," at least among clay enthusiasts. There were a few notable crossovers where painters made pots too. People like Miro and Picasso worked in the now glorified mud. Clay was popular. During this period only relative price and art history texts stood between painting and clay.

The end of the third quarter of the century was marked in 1977 by a watershed text by Harry Davis, "An Historical Review of Art Commerce and Craftsmanship."[1] Davis finally clarified what we had long understood, "That if you ignored status and price, the words craft and art had the same meaning," and therefore that, "Clay is art and art is craft." The last quarter century has seemed to bring a great frustration among clay users with the continuing disparity in price and prestige, and a frustration at the ineducability of the painting world. After all, they are trying to hang on to their economic might. The keynote address at the National Council on Education for the Ceramic Arts in 2002 by James Elkins[2] expressed the growing feeling of, "Who needs 'em." Now that the century is over, maybe the mood is, was, or should be, "Clay is not paint."

The lack of a one-to-one clay/painting relationship should be readily apparent. Although a few of us have made functional paintings, little consideration is given them by painters. We call our functional paintings "signs" and "oil cloths." This has been known to infuriate painters.

Painters have such a nice word for themselves: "painters." Potters have a similar word. Every time I utter "ceramic artist," I feel brittle. If you drop a couple of ceramic artists do they crack? We need a new word, and for lack of something better, I propose clayer. It's nice, short and easy to spell. If a painter uses paint, a clayer uses clay.

One could forgive the art historians. Clay just complicates the timeline. Where the main art historical stories of paint are chronological, those of clay are often technological. Where these stories of paint delve into non-Western art, either they cover the last 250 years or they never get past Iran and Egypt. Even the great Moslem empire in India is often left out. Ceramic history always bumps into Asia and the Middle East

Continued

and seems incomplete without good coverage of Central and South America. Either clayers have more worldwide importance than painters, or we are just more multiculturally aware and sensitive.

Similarly clayers often have the broadest definition of art. "Well hey, if a functional drinking vessel is art, how about my kiln?" From this widening descends a complete breakdown of the boundaries of the word "art." At least when we say clay, we know what it means.

Observation: Art's nose seems to be pointing a bit high in the air.

Background: The root of the word art, *ars,* means to put things together. This could be images, busts of Aristotle, or teapots that have been "put together." It could be ideas, computer programs or Hondas.

Definition: For me, the prime definition of art is: any artifact of intelligence.

Justification: The garbage man comes by your house. He had a bad night. He picks up your new, shining, galvanized can (All right, I'm a traditionalist, but it's not plastic.) turns it upside down into the truck, the garbage is stuck, nothing comes out. Did I mention that you're watching through the window and concerned about your new trashcan? You despise garbage men because they destroy your cans.

The garbage man (It could be a garbage woman, too.) had a bad eve-ning the night before, broke up with his partner, slams your brand new gleaming can on the side of the truck. Wham, Wham, Wham! He takes his frustration out on your can. Finally the recalcitrant garbage slides from the can. What have you witnessed? Is it expressive movement? Is that not dance? And the artifact, your tortured can, is it not a recording of human emotion. What does artifact mean?

The paint-centric world is caught up in a self-inflationary stance. My prime definition is seen as the pin in a room of balloons. It is a threat to money and status. I'll paraphrase the common view, "art is art unless it's clay; clay is craft." Paint fails to see great secrets we clayers hold close:

1. Pot-making is an incredibly formal pursuit involving proportion, form, movement and gesture, to name just a few such principles.

2. Abstract Expressionism in clay pre-dates Jackson Pollack by at least 250 years.

3. It helps if you know how to manipu-late your medium.

Ahrt! Just to say this word I some-times want to put on the English country gentleman's costume, the sports coat and tie. Art needs to amble off of his marble pedestal and think about climb-ing onto the dinner table.

1. *Studio Potter* magazine: Volume 6, Number 1, December, 1977, "An Historical Review of Art, Commerce and Crafts-manship," a lecture by New Zealand potter Harry Davis
2. *NCECA Journal* 2002, Volume XXIII, page 16, "Two Ways of Looking at Ceramics" by James Elkins

Jane Graber

Nashville, Indiana

"Americana Dreams II," 6.5 inches (17 cm) in height, 1-inch-scale wheel-thrown stoneware, cobalt stain, mahogany and basswood cabinet

"Americana Dreams I," 7.5 inches (19 cm) in height, 1-inch-scale (1 foot reproduced as 1 inch) wheel-thrown red earthenware with slip trailing and sgraffito, basswood cabinet

Juan Granados

Lubbock, Texas

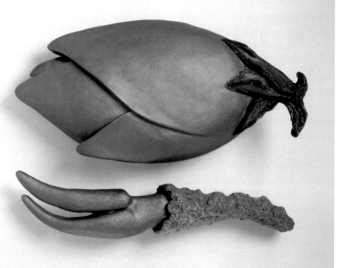

"Support," 27 inches (69 cm) in height, glazed earthenware, photo: Jon Q. Thompson

"Germination," 29 inches (74 cm) in height, glazed earthenware, photo: Jon Q. Thompson

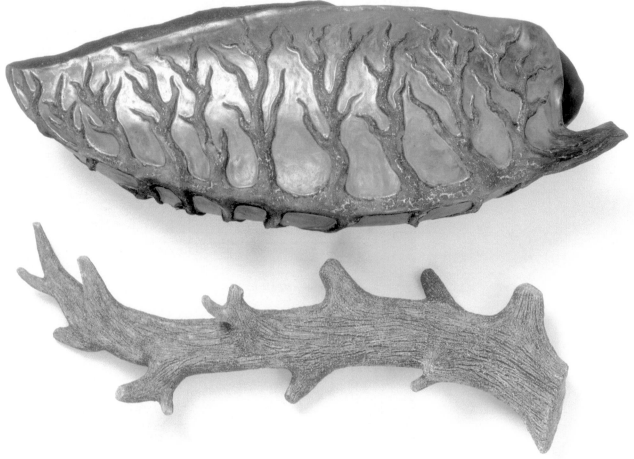

Bill Griffith

Gatlinburg, Tennessee

Photo: Jill Krzycki

"Dwelling #1," 15 inches (38 cm) in height, slab-built stoneware, wood-fired; on loan from the collection of Robyn and John Horn, photo: Jeff Brown

"Dwelling #2," 11 inches (28 cm) in height, slab-built stoneware, wood/salt-fired , photo: Jeff Brown

Chris Gustin

South Dartmouth Massachusetts

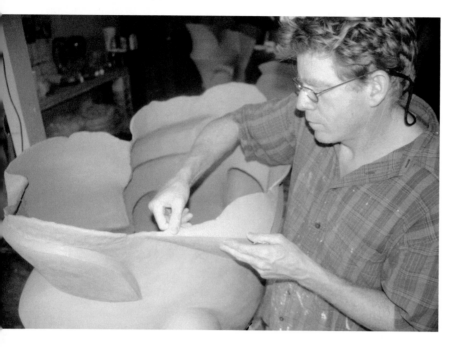

Vase, 29 inches (74 cm) in height, porcelain, wheel thrown and coiled, anagama fired, photo: Dean Powell

Bowl, 16 inches (41 cm) in height, porcelain, wheel thrown and coiled, reduction fired, photo: Dean Powell

"Zhong with Bufonidae,"
17.5 inches (44 cm) in
height, thrown black
stoneware with slips,
reduction cooled

"Flask with Armadillo," 9
inches (23 cm) in height,
handbuilt and press-
molded black stoneware
with slips, reduction cooled

Photos: R. W. Harrison

"Tapering Rectangular Clay Window," 13 inches (33 cm) in height, handbuilt, wood-fired porcelain with feldspar inclusions and gold luster

"Lotus-Arch Clay Window," 12 inches (30 cm) in height, handbuilt, wood-fired porcelain with feldspar inclusions and gold luster

Rebecca Harvey

Columbus, Ohio

"Marco/Polo," 9 inches (23 cm) in height, slip-cast, handbuilt and altered porcelain, photo: Rebecca Harvey

"Duck Stack," 12 inches (30 cm) in height, handbuilt and assembled porcelain, photo: Rebecca Harvey

Gwen Heffner

Irvine, Kentucky

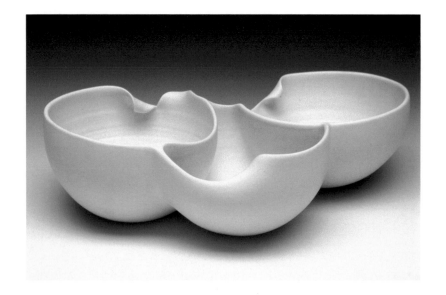

"Triplets," 4 inches (10 cm) in height, wheel-thrown porcelain, cut, joined and altered, oxidation fired to Cone 9, high-feldspar matt glaze, photo: Geoff Carr

"Gold Urchin Teapot," 10 inches (25 cm) in height, wheel-thrown porcelain, incised, slip trailed, with stain over glaze, oxidation fired to Cone 9, photo: Geoff Carr

"Revolution," 10 inches (25 cm) in height, clay,
cadmium over steel

"www.rack, 2000," 18 inches (46 cm) in width, clay, wood, Formica, photo: Tim Thayer

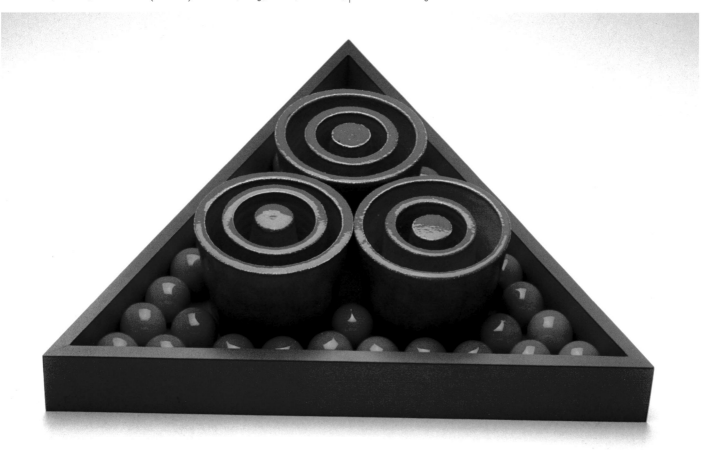

Mark Hewitt

Pitsboro, North Carolina

"Requiem Grave Marker," 29 inches (74 cm) in height, wood-fired stoneware, thrown, inscribed with the Latin requiem mass, salted ash glaze, photo: Jason Dowdle

"The Sultan's Two Lips (Large Vase)," 41 inches (104 cm) in height, wood-fired stoneware, thrown and coiled, salted ash glaze, incised, with blue glass runs, photo: Jason Dowdle

Catharine Hiersoux

Berkeley, California

Vase, 16 inches (41 cm) in height, wood-fired ceramics, photo: Richard Sargent

Vase, 16 inches (41 cm) in height, thrown and wood-fired ceramics, photo: Richard Sargent

Photos: Brian Ogelsbee

Wayne Higby

Alfred Station, New York

"Green River Gorge," 9 inches (23 cm) in height, earthenware, raku technique

"Fidolon Creek," 8 inches (20 cm) in height, earthenware, raku technique

Photos: Al Surratt

Melon Pitcher, 13 inches (33 cm) in height, thrown and altered stoneware, ribbed slip application, single fired

Bowl, 5 inches (13 cm) in height, thrown and altered stoneware, ribbed slip application, single fired

Chuck Hindes

Iowa City, Iowa

Wood-Fired Jar, 8 inches (20 cm) in height, handbuilt stoneware, natural ash deposits, photo: Chuck Hindes

Wood-Fired Tea Bowl, 5.25 inches (13 cm) in width, slipped stoneware, reduction cooled, photo: Chuck Hindes

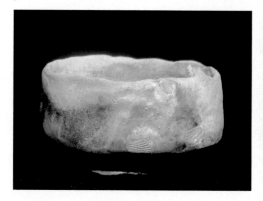

Photo: James R. Dean

Anne E. Hirondelle

Port Townsend, Washington

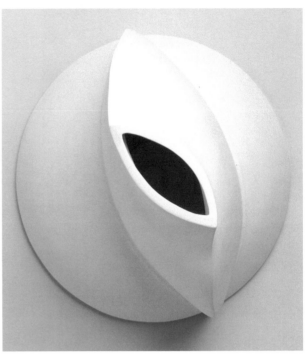

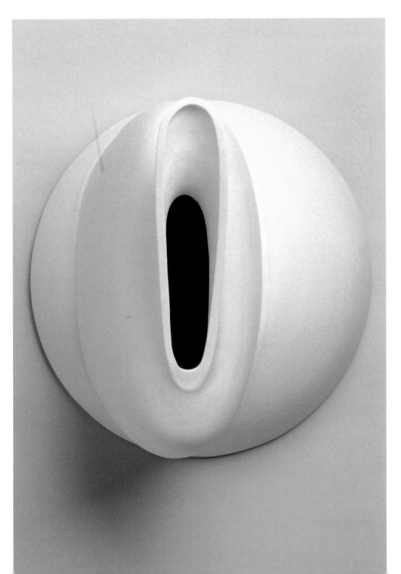

"Outurn 28," 12.5 inches (32 cm) in height, unglazed white stoneware, thrown and coil built, sanded and sealed, photo: Frank Ross

"Outurn 31," 12.5 inches (32 cm) in height, unglazed white stoneware, thrown and coil built, sanded and sealed, photo: Frank Ross

Rick Hirsch
Rochester, New York

Photo: Dan Rioz

"Mortar and Pestle #4," 16.25 inches (41 cm) in height; mortar: low fired slips and glazes; base: raku patination; pestle: white terra sigillatta, sawdust fired; photo: Geoff Tesch

"Altar Bowl # 35," 16.25 inches (41 cm) in height; bowl: wood-fired stoneware, salt fumed; base: raku patination; weapon: cast glass, sandblasted; photo: Geoff Tesch

Thomas Hoadley

Lanesboro, Massachusetts

"Untitled (#666)," 7.75 inches (20 cm) in
height, colored porcelain, unglazed, gold leaf

"Untitled (#616)," 6.25 inches (16 cm)
in height, colored porcelain, unglazed

Curtis Hoard

Minneapolis, Minnesoat

"Vase with Dog Figures," 30 inches (76 cm) in height, stoneware with Shino glaze and luster

"Vase with Bird and Figures," 30 inches (76 cm) in height, stoneware, soda fired with low-fire glaze

Patrick Horsley

Portland, Oregon

"T-pot/Purple," 21 inches (53 cm) in height, thrown and altered stoneware, photo: Courtney Frisse

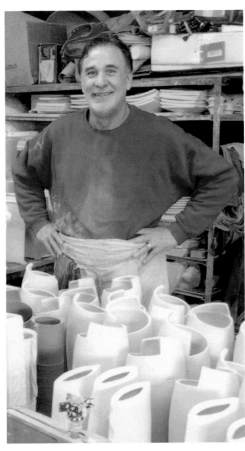

"Boat Vase," 10 inches (25 cm) in height, thrown and altered stoneware, photo: Courtney Frisse

Teapot, 6 inches (15 cm) in height, thrown, wood-fired stoneware with brushed white slip

Small Storage Jar, 7 inches (18 cm) in height, thrown, wood-fired stoneware with fly ash deposits

Photos: John Cummings

Sylvia Hyman

Nashville, Tennessee

"Tomato Box with Blueprints," 9.5 inches (24 cm) in height, handbuilt stoneware and porcelain, screenprinted

"Crate of Books and Things," 10 inches (25 cm) in height, handbuilt, stoneware and porcelain

Sarah Jaeger

Helena, Montana

Tureen and Tray, 9 inches (23 cm) in height, wheel-thrown porcelain, glazed, with wax resist, oxidation fired in a gas kiln

Bowl, 13 inches (33 cm) in diameter, wheel-thrown porcelain with trailed glaze decoration, reduction fired, photo: Doug O'Looney

Randy Johnston

River Falls, Wisconsin

"Boat Form", 8 inches (20 cm) in height,
wood fired with kaolin slip,
photo: Peter Lee

"Vase Form," 16 inches (41 cm) in height,
wood-fired kaolin slip,
photo: Peter Lee

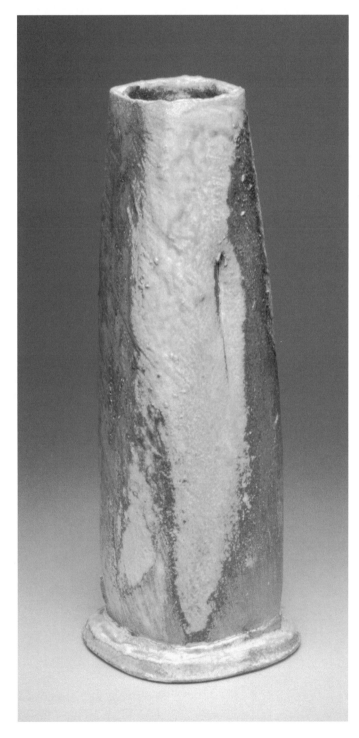

"Recumbent Batter Bowl," 14 inches (36 cm) in height, soda-fired stoneware with Devore and Ranger wash

"Recumbent Bowl," 15 inches (38 cm) in height, soda-fired stoneware with Devore and Ranger wash

Diane Kenney

Carbondale, Colorado

Covered Jar, 11 inches (28 cm) in height, wheel-thrown porcelain with incised slip exterior, soda/salt fired

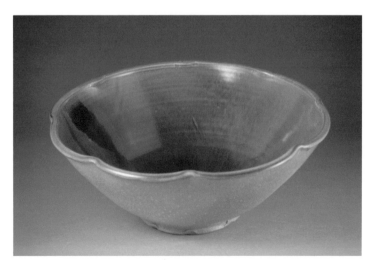

Serving Bowl, 5 inches (13 cm) in height, wheel-thrown porcelain, glazed slip interior, incised, soda/salt fired

Tom Kerrigan

Tucson, Arizona

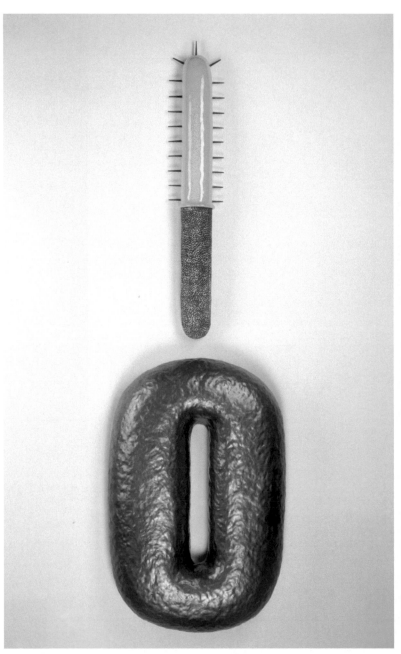

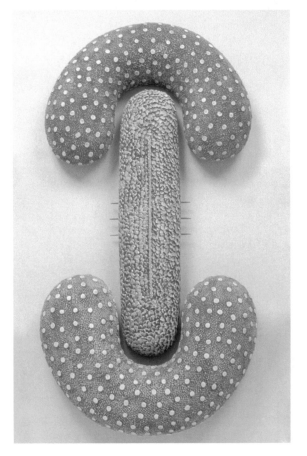

"Desert Flora XXII," 57 inches (145 cm) in height, handbuilt earthenware with glaze, stain, and metal

"Desert Flora XV," 48 inches (122 cm) in height, handbuilt earthenware with glaze, stain, and metal

"Ice and Water Series 0303," 20 inches (51 cm) in height, handbuilt stoneware with melted glass, fired to Cone 7, photo: Y. C. Kim

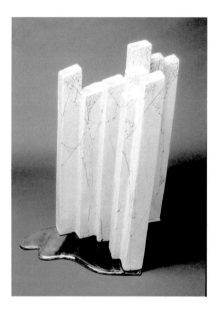

"Melting Away: 0208," 10 inches (25 cm) in height, stoneware with lichen glaze and melted glass, fired to Cone 7, photo: Y. C. Kim

"The Great Experiment 2001, 911 Homage to America," 137 inches (348 cm) in height, architectural ceramics

"Templo De Martes, 2001," 137 inches (348 cm) in height, architectural ceramics

"Heavenly Dish," 17.5 inches (44 cm) in height, thrown, slip-cast white earthenware with majolica glaze and china paints, photo: Leigh Rabby

"Arachnid Coleomegilla Mania," 18 inches (46 cm) in height, thrown, press-molded white earthenware with majolica glaze and china paints, photo: Leigh Rabby

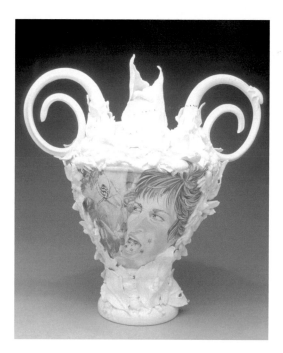

Paul Kotula

Huntington Woods, Michigan

Vase with Handles, 13.25 inches (34 cm) in height, handbuilt stoneware, photo: Jim Thayer

Place Setting, 5 inches (13 cm) in height, stoneware, porcelain, wood, press-molded plate, handbuilt bowl, found small plate, photo: Jim Thayer

Eva Kwong

Kent, Ohio

Photo: Kirk Mangas

"Dark Glow Vase," 12 inches (30 cm) in height, wheel-thrown and assembled stoneware with colored slips and salt glaze

"Big Blue Vase," 8.5 inches (22 cm) in height, wheel-thrown and assembled stoneware with colored slips and salt glaze

"Ginger Jar Tandem," 12 inches (30 cm) in height,
wood-fired porcelain

Teapot with Plate, 8 inches (20 cm) in height, wood-fired porcelain

Julie & Tyrone Larson

Asheville, North Carolina

Photo: Joe Gurdal

"Italian Platter," 17.25 inches (44 cm) in width, thrown porcelain by Tyrone Larson; glaze painting by Julie Larson, photo: Tim Barnwell

"Gothic Carrots," 13 inches (33 cm) in width, thrown porcelain by Tyrone Larson; glaze painting by Julie Larson, photo: Tim Barnwell

Jaye Lawrence

El Cajon, California

"Small Seated Figure," 18 inches (46 cm) in height, clay, wood, wire, paint

"Seated Figure," 54 inches (137 cm) in height, clay, wood, wire, paint

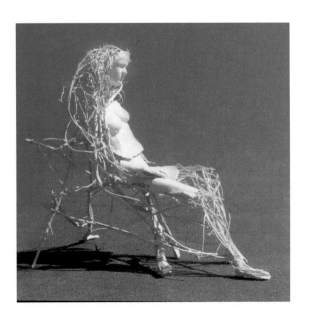

A Note from New York City

Neil Tetkowski

I write this chapter for *21st Century Ceramics in the United States and Canada* from my studio in New York City, looking out the window to West 18th Street. The largest concentration of art galleries in North America, and perhaps the world, is just a five-minute walk from here. The first few begin right on this block. It is a staggering thought that while there are more than 100 art galleries in the Chelsea neighborhood of the city, the harsh reality is that only a tiny percentage will ever show art made of clay. The myth that New York City is the epicenter of the art world still rings true, but...when will New York celebrate art about nature or art made of clay?

It all makes sense if you consider that a typical New Yorker's zest for life is not about nature or the earth. It is clearly about something else, for no one I know ever moved to the Big Apple for health or for fresh air. So it should be no surprise that the focus of art shown in most museums and galleries is now technology driven. I call it funhouse art. These installations in darkened galleries make noise, have moving parts, video projections and flashing lights. You are bound to see these imaginative works featured at important taste-making shows like the Whitney Biennial. Marshall McLuhan was a true prophet when he said, "the media is the message." Media have taken over, not just in the art world but in the world of politics as well. This is truly the trend of our times.

Nevertheless, there are plenty of exceptions that keep the art world interesting. In fact, at the Whitney Museum there is a permanently installed Charles Simmons ceramic work tucked into a peculiar space, albeit the stair-

well. Andy Goldsworthy enjoys a well-deserved yet remarkable popularity in this contemporary context; and Isamu Noguchi is having an important exhibition of his ceramics at the Smithsonian in D.C. Admittedly the audience for clay continues to grow but is limited by collective imagination and reality. For example, the American Craft Museum will soon reopen with a new name and a new identity in a new building. The "C" word was eliminated and now it is officially called the Museum of Arts and Design, i.e. MAD. MOMA has some random ceramics in the Design and Architecture department but isn't planning any clay exhibitions that I know about. Sometimes behind the ticket counter you will see a colorful Betty Woodman vase filled with fresh cut flowers to grace the entryway.

In the early days of New York City there were a few potters with studios in what is now the Wall Street area. Today it is a striking fact that there are hundreds of enthusiastic artists working in clay throughout the five boroughs of the city and there are many schools where one can take classes. It is truly inspiring to see how many talented people figure out a way to do their work and still enjoy this amazing mix of humanity. In this vast city there is a lot happening in clay. At any given moment there are several shows somewhere in the city featuring ceramics. And if you go for a walk you are bound to find clay where you least expect it; in random shops, galleries and restaurants. But the most expensive ceramics are not on the auction block at Sotheby's. Instead, they are right on the street. I'm talking New York real estate. More than half of the buildings here are made of fired clay but you couldn't touch a little brick garage for a cool million. There's your irony for the day.

"New Vision Tea Pot #A030502," 8 inches (20 cm) in height, oxidation-fired porcelain, photo-silkscreen monoprint, stainless steel, photo: Les Lawrence

"New Vision Tea Pot #A030402," 8 inches (20 cm) in height, oxidation-fired porcelain, photo-silkscreen monoprint, stainless steel, photo: Les Lawrence

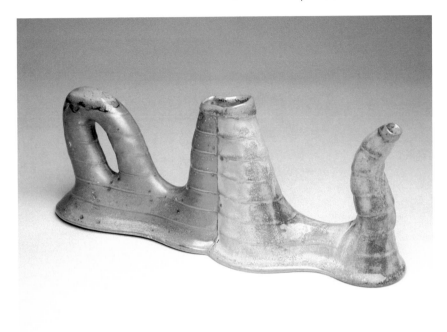

"Bisected Teapot," 6 inches (15 cm) in height, thrown and altered, salt-glazed stoneware

Double Handle Covered Jar, 13 inches (33 cm) in height, thrown and altered, salt-glazed stoneware, photo: James Lawton

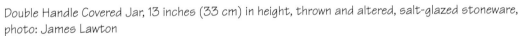

"Taste of Lime," 6.75 inches (17 cm) in width, slab-built, Cone 10 soda-fired ceramics with glaze inlay and incising

"Marijke," 10 inches (25 cm) in width, slab-built, Cone 10 reduction-fired ceramics with glaze inlay

Dick Lehman

Goshen, Indiana

Wood-Fired Jar, 12 inches (30 cm) in height, fired for 12 days with Chinese Elm fuel; all-natural ash glaze, photo: Dick Lehman

Wood-Fired Bottle, 15 inches (38 cm) in height, fired for 12 days with Chinese elm fuel; all-natural ash glaze, photo: Dick Lehman

Photo: Howard Zehr

"White Wheel, Kosmos Series," 12 inches (30 cm) in height, porcelaneous carving, photo: Eva Heyd

"Westerwald Hemisphere," 10 inches (25 cm) in height, white stoneware fired in Westerwald-style (wood-fired salt) kiln in Germany

Photo: Neil Tetkowski

Marilyn Levine

Oakland, California

"Meister," 5.5 inches (14 cm) in height, high-fire ceramics with fabric shoelace, photo: Richard Sargent

"Nitro," 5.25 inches (13 cm) in height, high-fire ceramics with fabric shoelace, photo: Richard Sargent

Daniel Levy
New York, New York

Oval Bowl, 15 inches (38 cm) in width, slip-cast porcelain with colored slips under a satin glaze with platinum luster fired on the rim

Tray with Pitcher and Cups, the pitcher is 6 inches (15 cm) in height, all are slip-cast porcelain with colored slips under glaze with 22K gold on the rim

Paul Lewing

Seattle, Washington

"Mount Rainer/Fields Trivet," 14 inches (36 cm) in height, porcelain tile with Cone 4 glazes, extruded border

"Spray Park/Mount Rainer," 26 inches (66 cm) in height, porcelain tile with Cone 4 glazes, extruded border

Suze Lindsay

Bakersville, North Carolina

"Stacked Bouquet With Feet," 13 inches (33 cm) in height, thrown and altered stoneware, paddled feet, slip decorated, salt fired to Cone 10, photo: Tom Mills

Footed Teapot, 10.25 inches (26 cm) in height, handbuilt and thrown stoneware elements, assembled, slip decorated, salt fired to Cone 10, photo: Tom Mills

Mitch Lyons

New London, Pennsylvasnia

"Test Ring," 14 inches (36 cm) in height, colored clay print from a slab of 23-year-old clay

"Eutectic," 13 inches (33 cm) in height, colored-clay print from a slab of wet clay

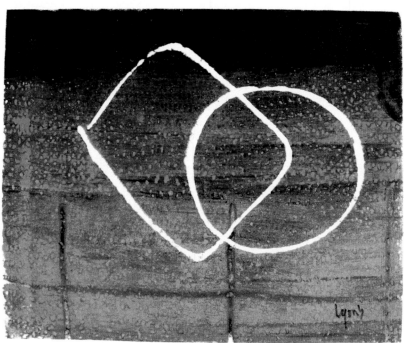

Marilyn Lysohir

Moscow, Idaho

Marilyn Lysohir with "The Tattooed Ladies and the Dinosaur," 41 inches (104 cm) in height, handbuilt ceramic legs with terra sigillata and underglaze wax; press-molded ceramic bones with Cone 6 and 04 glazes, photo: Mark La Moreaux

"Tiles from the Tattooed Ladies," 12 inches (30 cm) in height, earthenware with Cone 04 underglazes, photo: Mark La Moreaux

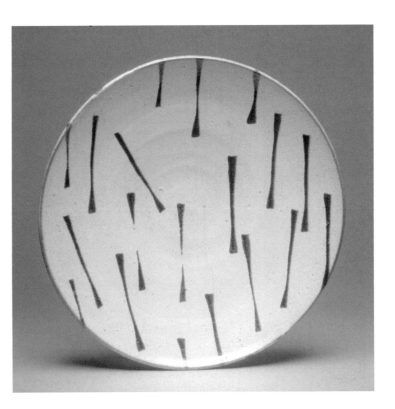

Warren MacKenzie

Stillwater, Minnesota

Platter, 19 inches (48 cm) in diameter, thrown, glazed stoneware, photo: Peter Lee

Covered Pot, 14 inches (36 cm) in height, thrown and fluted stoneware, photo: Peter Lee

Peg Malloy

Carbondale, Colorado

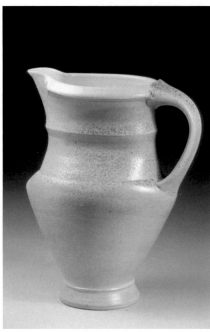

"Corsetta Pitcher," 10 inches (25 cm) in height, thrown in two sections altered and assembled, pulled handle, Shino slip applied at bone dry stage, fired 17 days in a Bourry box kiln

Altered Bowl, 9.5 inches (24 cm) in width, thrown and altered, Shino slip applied when bone dry, fired 17 hours in a Bourry box (self-stoking) wood kiln

"Bowl with Cutouts," 16.5 inches (42 cm) in width, white stoneware, fired at Cone 6, photo: Rick Malmgren

"Lava Spikes Vase," 17 inches (43 cm) in height, white stoneware, fired at Cone 6 in reduction, photo: Rick Malmgren

Tom Malone

Heyworth Illinois

"Tea for Friends,"
10.5 inches (27 cm)
in height, thrown
stoneware with slips,
salt-glazed

"Food for Friends,"
11.5 inches (29 cm)
in height, thrown
stoneware with slips,
salt-glazed

Ginny Marsh

Rockwell, Texas

Photo: Janet Haig

Bottle, 6.5 inches (17 cm) in height, pinch pot, slab-built porcelain, raku fired, with post-firing reduction, celadon glaze, photo: Bradley Chrisenberry

Platter, 14 inches (36 cm) in diameter, thrown stoneware with white slip over leaf stencils, Shino-type glaze, reduction fired to Cone 9, photo: Bradley Chrisenberry

Craig Martell

Salem, Oregon

Porcelain Platter, 20 inches (51 cm) in height, wheel thrown, slip decorated with temmoku and ash glazes, Cone 10 reduction fired, photo: Bill Bachhuber

Bowl with Cut Rim, 8 inches (20 cm) in height, wheel-thrown porcelain, slip decorated with temmoku and ash glazes, Cone 10 reduction fired, photo: Bill Bachhuber

Karen Thuesen Massaro

Santa Cruz, California

"Garden Line," 5 inches (13 cm) in height, assembled, slip-cast porcelain elements, underglaze, glaze, fired to Cone 10, with Cone 017 multifired china paint, photo: Paul Schraub

"Kiwi," 7.5 inches (19 cm) in height, assembled, slip-cast porcelain elements, underglaze, glaze, fired to Cone 10, with Cone 017 multifired china paint, photo: Paul Schraub

Tim Mather

Bloomington, Indiana

"WIGFY #22", 14 inches (36 cm) in height, multi-fired and assembled slip-cast ceramics

"WIGFY #27", multi-fired and assembled slip-cast ceramics

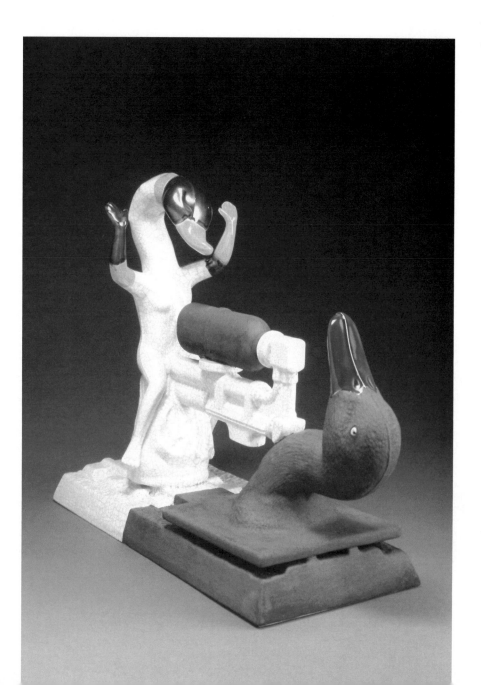

"Oh My Gosh, Its A Love Shrine," 21.5 inches (55 cm) in height, thrown and handbuilt, soda-fired earthenware, photo: George McCauley

"Oh Look, Its the Blue Goddess," 16 inches (41 cm) in height, thrown and handbuilt, soda-fired earthenware, photo: George McCauley

Photo: Vince Pitelka

Photo: Bayard Morgan

Wood-fired Vase, 9 inches (23 cm)
in height, slab built, wood fired,
photo: Peter Lee

Spouted Bowl, 4 inches (10 cm) in
height, thrown with added spout,
wood fired, photo: Peter Lee

"Plate with Window," 30 inches (76 cm) in diameter, incised redware with slips

Plate with Head," 30 inches (76 cm) in diameter, incised redware with slips

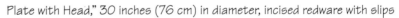

Jim Melchert

Oakland, California

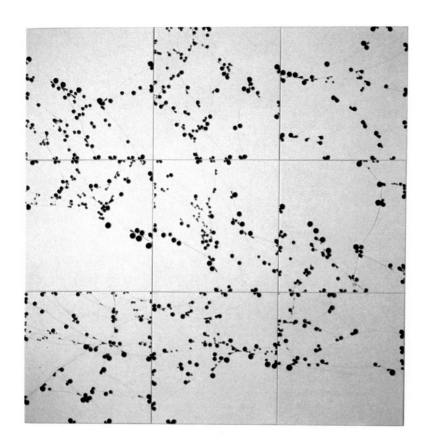

"November Yield," 52.25 inches (133 cm) in height, glaze on tile, photo: Lee Fatheree

"Small Yield #2, 2001," 23.5 inches (60 cm) in height, glaze on porcelain tile, photo: Lee Fatheree

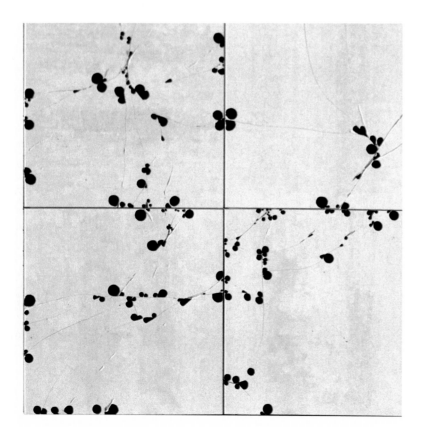

Matthew Metz

Houston, Minnesota

Box, 9 inches (23 cm) in height, wood-fired and salt-glazed porcelain with terra sigillata and sgraffito, photo: Peter Lee

Pitcher, 15 inches (38 cm) in height, wood-fired and salt-glazed porcelain and stoneware combined, photo: Peter Lee

Ron Meyers

Athens, Georgia

Platter, 18 inches (46 cm) in diameter, earthenware with underglaze and transparent glaze, photo: Walker Montgomery

Teapot, 12 inches (30 cm) in height, soda-fired earthenware, photo: Walker Montgomery

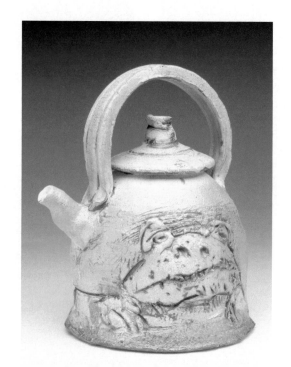

Les Miley

Evansville, Indiana

Altered Jar with Lid, 9.5 inches (24 cm) in height, wheel-thrown, salt-glazed stoneware with rutile slip and cobalt ash glaze

Wood-Fired Porcelain Lidded Jar, 9 inches (23 cm) in height, wheel-thrown porcelain, wood fired to Cone 9-10, photo: Peg Malloy

Gifford Myers

Altadena, California

"Cup 'O' Toscana," 12 inches (30 cm) in height, glazed ceramics on lacquered mount

"The Furthest Way about is the Nearest Way Home," 36 inches (91cm) in length, raku, from raw clay to glaze

Mark Nafziger

Archbold, Ohio

"...and the Big One Got Away," 17 inches (43 cm) in diameter, thrown stoneware with slip trailing, Cone 10 reduction fired

"Fan Grid," 15.5 inches (39 cm) in diameter, thrown stoneware with slip trailing, Cone 10 reduction fired

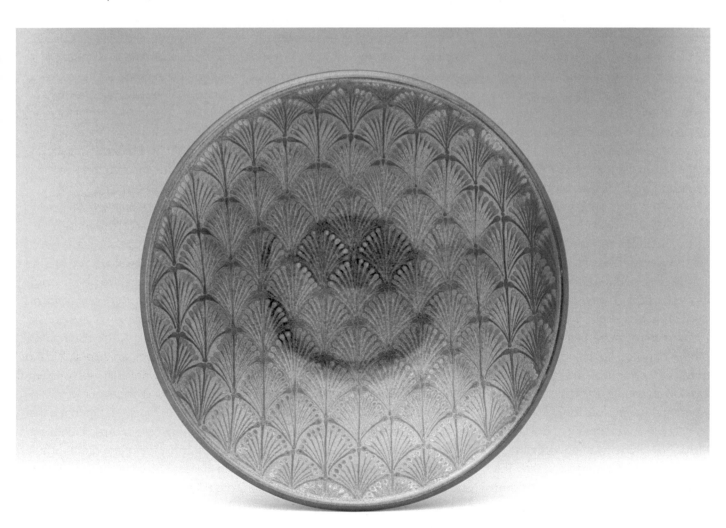

More Tangible than Technique,

More Timeless than Age

Dick Lehman

"How many of you, if your lives depended on it, could make and successfully fire a figure the size and complexity of one of these Chinese terracotta warriors or horses?," asked Professor Randy Schmidt. Not a hand went up among this group of Arizona State University graduate students.

He continued, "Here we are in the late 20th century, with perhaps more printed information about ceramics than at any other time in history: more tools, more techniques, more clays, better kilns, more museums. We think we are pretty hot stuff. Yet not one of us is willing to stake our lives on being able to make works of similar complexity and scale, beauty and power, compared to the work that those ceramic artists of more than 2000 years ago were routinely producing."

In the years since my visiting artist stint at ASU, I've held onto Schmidt's questions and observations. His questions may have been thinly veiled indictments, and were surely meant to motivate second semester graduate students to get serious and to make the best use of the resources that were at their disposal. But his observations about lost skills, and works of long-lasting power, beauty and conviction were what most stayed with me.

Last week I ate out of a "Kitchen Ming" bowl from my small collection. It is a bowl that just begs to be used. The dingy foot belies a decade of decades of use. The family name of perhaps the first of its many owners is scratched

through the glaze in the center of the bowl right next to the unglazed ring where the foot of the next bowl sat atop this one; just one of many in the stack; one of many stacks in many kilns in many firings. Balancing the foot of the bowl on three fingers of my left hand, I gave the rim a sharp tap. The bell-clear-ring lasted for four seconds; certainly as clear and true today as it was the day it was unloaded from the kiln more than 100 years ago. What a remarkable clay body! In all my years of body tests, I've never developed anything comparable to this "common" body. And I'm not sure I'd stake my life on being able to do so. But more importantly, this simple bowl has a convincing resonance of utility that has stood the test of time.

Recently a potter-friend sent me the image of an 1830s John Lehman alkaline-glazed jar with its robust 6- to 8-gallon capacity and its confident self-disclosing sculptural relief decoration right above the bold signature on the side of the pot. These details indicate a casual yet refined competence. And although we share the same last name, and perhaps the same Swiss-German ancestry (and quite possibly even the same DNA), I doubt that I could reproduce what "uncle John" created almost 200 years ago. My friend noted that the auction estimate is set at somewhere near $70,000. More than age or rarity is at auction here: Uncle John's humanity speaks through the sculpting, telling us, perhaps, something of his artistic inheritance, his politics, his theology, his imagination and his dreams; communicating clearly through all these years the things he

held most dear. That, I suspect, is what the bidders are buying.

The Jomon era shard that I nervously fingered last week was made sometime around the 4th or 3rd-millennium B.C.E. The shard is small enough that its role as part of a vessel or sculpture is obscured. The casual, almost playful, assurance of decoration indicate that this was not the first piece this clay artist had made. A clear and purposeful pattern is lined out with alternating swift gouges, playing against lines that were formed by repeatedly pressing a pointed stick into the clay while skillfully guiding the stick along.

The time and care invested in this shard cause me to surmise that it was not simply made for the maker's own sake. The skill and care imply relationships. The time that it takes to be so purposeful implies a secure and nurturing set of relationships: a society that produced the economy of leisure this design requires.

And whether this small shard was part of a sculptural form whose function was tied to symbols, rituals, beliefs and values; or if it was part of a vessel whose function was directed toward containment or storage or serving; or if it was simply a function of egocentric personal expression...I couldn't guess. All these functions are essential, in that they capture what is simplest and what is most profound about our living. So it does not so much matter to me that I can't determine its explicit function. What matters is that the grace and playfulness and assurance in this shard are still powerful and convincing, more than 5000 years after my ceramic ancestor left his or her finger marks on it. And placing my fingerprints along-side hers — apart from being an almost sacred experience — causes me to wonder: Will our work stand the same test of time; not just physically surviving, but communicating clearly too? Will it leave clues about beliefs and values, about economy and intentions and relationships?

I suppose all of us who love the ceramic arts have shared similar experiences, encountering works that engender awe and wonder. We are so fortunate to live in a time when we need travel only a few miles to see, first hand, fine examples of 12th century Persian luster ware, or pre-Columbian sculpture stretching back to our 7000 B.C. aboriginal soul-mates, or the remarkable Sèvres porcelains, or the too-long-overlooked masterpieces of American Indians. Indeed, in this time of unparalleled access through the Internet, at our slightest whim, examples of all of these and more come almost instantly to us in our homes or schools or studios.

But it is neither the sometimes-lost techniques that set the best of these works apart, nor simply their age. The most powerful of these works carry with-in themselves something more tangible than technique, more timeless than age. Like good poetry, they speak the language of the soul, capturing and re-flecting both the simplest and the most profound meanings of existence.

Now, personally, I believe that ceramists in the 21st century can be forgiven for not knowing how to sculpt those 300 B.C.E. terracotta horses. We need not confine ourselves to being the technical sum of all previous ceramic generations. And there is no particu-lar merit in ceramic ventriloquism. We have, after all, our own work to do, our own voices to speak. (And if it is impor-tant to learn to make terracotta horses, we can probably do so.)

But as for continuing through our own work to speak the language of the soul, to that we have an obligation.

And for its omission, there can be no excuse.

How then, as 21st century ce-ramists, do we speak the language of the soul? How do we create works of long-lasting power and beauty and conviction? Will our work reflect both the simplest and the most profound meanings of our living?

Of course these are inquiries that we must attempt to address for ourselves. And the measuring of our success may well be left to those who follow after us. But I would expect that these more ultimate inquiries would include some reflection upon at least a portion of the following questions:

Did we maintain a connection to our culture without simply reflecting it? Did our work challenge or reinvent culture? Were we informed enough and free enough to appropriate impor-tant elements from other cultures? Did our work speak to whatever was the current art movement without merely mouthing its precepts? Did we follow our hearts and singular visions even if the resulting work didn't fit into any movement? Did our work occupy a thoughtful, reflective, humorous, and perhaps even an irreverent or provoca-tive presence?

Did we work to maintain the openness and sharing that has already characterized at least portions of the worldwide ceramics community? And did we respect and learn from the ceramic traditions that, either through abuse or neglect, we may have previ-ously sidelined or ignored? Through our work, did we increase the inclusive na-ture of the field so that the unnecessary boundaries of gender, ethnicity, class and nationality do not define the field? Did we take a stance of "generativity" toward future generations of ceramic artists, in a manner that would encour-age them to surpass us, all the while expecting no less of ourselves?

Did we use the body of our life's work to address the most important political discourse of the day? Did

we use our lives and work to attempt to correct the increasing disparities of wealth and power, or were our works simply products for consumption by those who already have the most of everything? Were we able to address such serious questions without being overwhelmed by them? And did our work maintain space for some lighter fare? Did our works take advantage of clay's potential to address the deep and abiding connections to the com-mon fabric of daily life? Did we make room for the playful and humorous, the trivial and frivolous, the experimental or seemingly pointless? Did we value the media's potential to connect as well as to correct?

Did we use our sculpture and tiles, our assemblages and vessels to enhance, enrich and engender the best relationships of caring, trust and nurture? Did we neither overempha-size nor avoid clay's potential to focus on ourselves, our self-expression or our self-realization? Did we acknowledge our indebtedness to all those who have gone before us?

I imagine the central challenge for clay artists in the 21st century won't be primarily technical. The real chal-lenge, I suspect, will be to live up to the tradition of the best ceramic work of the past; making, for *our* time, tangible works that fulfill all the functions clay-work can address. This includes works of long-lasting power, beauty and con-viction. In short, we must address the timeless.

On the one hand, speaking the language of the soul is intensely personal, quietly elusive and terribly dif-ficult to define. Yet, making work that celebrates and contributes to justice and playfulness, mystery and openness, newness and beauty can also be de-ceptively simple...tantalizingly tangible. This essential pursuit contains a winsome but awkward paradox. But the most timeless things always do.

Andy Nasisse

Athens, Georgia

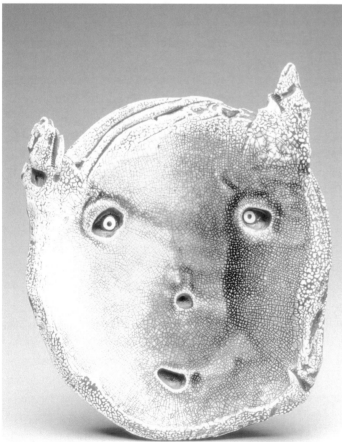

Covered Jar, 11 inches (28 cm) in height, multifired earthenware

"Face Plate," 12 inches (30 cm) in height, multifired earthenware

John Neely

Logan, Utah

Black Teapot, 7.5 inches (19 cm) in height, thrown and assembled stoneware with cane handle

Red Teapot, 7.5 inches (19 cm) in height, thrown and assembled stoneware with cane handle

Richard Notkin

Helena, Montana

Photo: Phoebe R. Toland

"Heart Teapot: The Pump II" (Yixing Series), 6.125 inches (16 cm) in height, handbuilt and assembled stoneware; courtesy of Garth Clark Gallery, NYC; photo: Richard Notkin

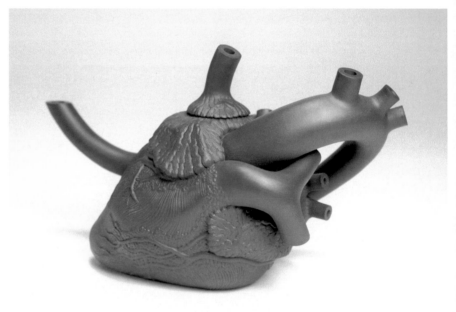

"Four Tiles (After Michelangelo): Studies for 'Progress'," 11.5 inches (29 cm) in width, terracotta with painted wood frame (frame not shown), number 2 in an edition of 10; courtesy of Garth Clark Gallery, NYC; photo: Richard Notkin

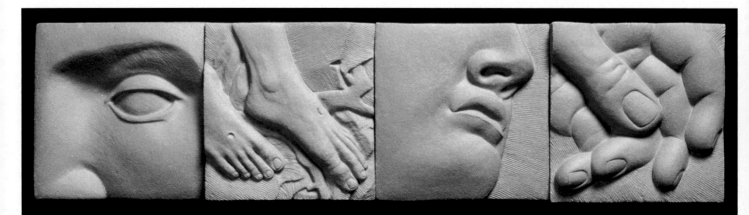

Sake Set, 8 inches (20 cm) in height, thrown and handbuilt, porcelain and stoneware, soda fired

Garnish Set, 6 inches (15 cm) in height, thrown and handbuilt, porcelain and stoneware, soda fired

Jeff Oestreich

Taylors Falls, Minnesota

Beaked Pitcher, 11 inches (28 cm) in height, thrown and altered, soda-fired stoneware, photo: Jeff Oestreich

Bowl, 5 inches (13 cm) in height, thrown and faceted stoneware, photo: Jeff Oestreich

"Twilight Reflections," 18 inches (46 cm) in height, Cone 5 clay, colored slips, glaze and Cone 5 overglaze, photo: Jeanne Otis

"Dark Passage, Pearl Light," 19.5 inches (50 cm) in height, Cone 5 clay, colored slips, glaze and Cone 5 overglaze, photo: Jeanne Otis

Photo: Bob Fronske

Ben Owen, 111

Seagrove, North Carolina

"Chinese Blue Han Vase," 10.5 inches (27 cm) in height, thrown, wood-fired stoneware, photo: David Ramsey

"Melon Vases," 11 inches (28 cm) in height, thrown, Shino-glazed stoneware, wood fired, photo: Juan Villa

Photo: David Ramsey

Photo: Philip Taylor

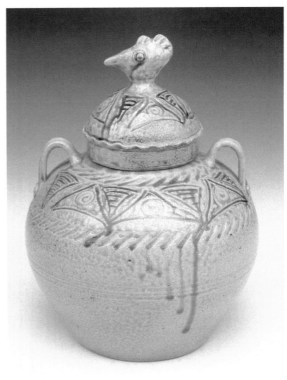

"Chicken Lidded Jar," 11 inches (28 cm) in height, thrown jar with molded chicken head, wood fired and salt glazed, photo: Jason Dowdle

"Teapot in Frogskin Glaze with Copper Handle," 8 inches (20 cm) in height, thrown, wood fired and salt glazed (handle made by Jennie Lorette Keatts), photo: Jason Dowdle

Vernon Owens

Seagrove, North Carolina

Wine Jug, 7.5 inches (19 cm) in height, stoneware with soft cobalt and copper glaze, wood fired and salt glazed, photo: Jason Dowdle

Jar, 12.5 inches (32 cm) in height, wheel-thrown stoneware, cobalt glaze with copper overdip, photo: Jason Dowdle

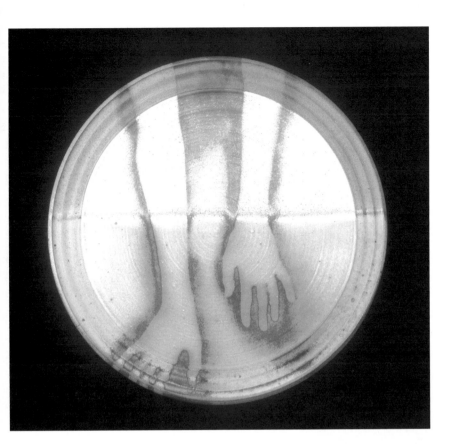

"Footfalls Echo in the Memory," 20 inches (51 cm) in width, stoneware glazed raw and fired with crankcase oil; color comes from dusted copper ore over a high calcium glaze, fired to Cone 10, photo: Valerie Parks

"Love Among the Ruins," 20 inches (51 cm) in width, stoneware glazed raw and fired with crankcase oil; color comes from dusted copper ore over a high calcium glaze, fired to Cone 10, photo: Valerie Parks

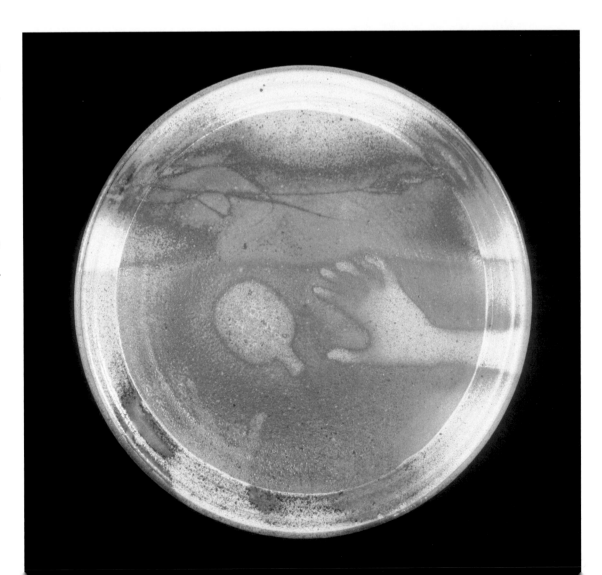

Rina Peleg

New York, New York

"Earth Carpet 2002 Installation", 48 inches (122 cm) in width, hand-woven ceramic tiles, underglaze and crackled glaze, photo: Rina Peleg

"American Flag 2001 Floor Installation", 60 inches (152 cm) in width, hand-woven ceramic tiles, underglaze and crackle glaze, photo: Jams Dine

"Tell (Philomla) 2002," 42 inches (107 cm) in height, handbuilt terracotta
with lowfire glaze and china paint; scarves, ceramic doorknobs, key, photo:
Roger Schreiber

John Peterson

Albany, Indiana

Covered Jar, 4.25 inches (11 cm) in height, thrown
salt-glazed stoneware with heavy slip

Vessel, 9.25 inches (23 cm) in height, thrown and altered, salt-glazed
stoneware with heavy slip

Photo: Mike Statler

Tom Phardel

Ann Arbor, Michigan

"Binou," 24 inches (61 cm) in height, salt-fired stoneware, steel, glass, and oil

"Bi-Lobe," 8 inches (20 cm) in height, salt-fired stoneware with crackle slip and glaze, photo: R.H. Hensleigh

Mark Pharis

Minneapolis, Minnesota

Vase, 20 inches (51 cm) in height, handbuilt earthenware, photo: Peter Lee

Teapot, 7 inches (18 cm) in height, handbuilt earthenware, photo: Peter Lee

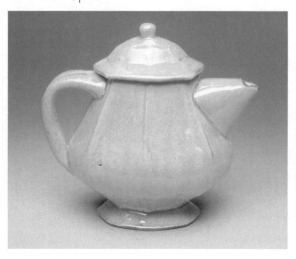

Todd Piker

Cornwall Bridge, Connecticut

2-Quart Casserole, 7 inches (18 cm) in height, wood-fired stoneware, light salt glaze

"2-Gallon Pitcher, North Devon Style," 12 inches (30 cm) in height, wood-fired stoneware, light salt glaze

Don Pilcher

Champaign, Illinois

"Orebowl 1," 5.5 inches (14 cm) in height, thrown and altered porcelain

"Orebowl 2," 5 inches (13 cm) in height, thrown and altered porcelain

"Wheat Stubble (Cup and Saucer)", 4 inches (10 cm) in height, soda-fired stoneware, thrown and altered

"Crosshatach (Cup and Saucer)", 4 inches (10 cm) in height, soda-fired stoneware, thrown and altered

"Oil Can #12," 24 inches (61 cm) in height, slab-built stoneware with laminated colored clays, soda fired to Cone 6

"Oil Storage Can #3," 24 inches (61 cm) in height, slab-built stoneware with laminated colored clays, soda fired to Cone 6

Photo: June Tessel

Greg Pitts

Brooklyn, New York

"Flower Brick #2," 5.5 inches (14 cm) in height, terracotta with sgraffito, lead glazed, photo: D. James Dean

"Flower Brick #1," 5.5 inches (14 cm) in height, terracotta with sgraffito, lead glazed, photo: D. James Dean

"Twins," 26 inches (66 cm) in height, stoneware, Cone 9 reduction fired

"Blue Plate Special," 11.5 inches (29 cm) in height, slab-built ceramics, Cone 3 reduction-fired matt glazes

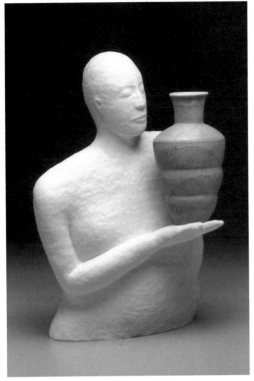

"Vase Fresh from the Kiln," 21 inches (53 cm) in height, white stoneware coil-built figure with thrown porcelain vase, photo: Tim Barnwell

Photo: Jeri Rodgers

"Woman with Tulip Vase," 19 inches (48 cm) in height, white stoneware coil-built figure with thrown porcelain vase, photo: Tim Barnwell

Rick Pope

Bozeman, Montana

Ceramic Form, 24 inches (61 cm) in height, stoneware, Shino glaze, wood fired

Ceramic Form, 30 inches (76 cm) in height, stoneware, Shino glaze, wood fired, photo: Dean Adams

"Josephyllus Mediopictus," 19 inches (48 cm) in height, coil built with mosaics, Cone 4 glazed with unglazed terracotta

"Rectus Globosus Eruptus," 25 inches (64 cm) in height, coil built with mosaics, glazed terracotta with terra sigillata

Photo: Dan Milner

Liz Quackenbush

Pleasant Gap, Pennsylvania

Goat, 28 inches (71 cm) in height, slab-built terracotta, majolica glaze with gold luster, photo: Dick Ackley

Chicken, 18 inches (46 cm) in height, slab-built terracotta, majolica glaze with gold lustre, photo: Dick Ackley

Will Ruggles & Douglass Rankin

Plate, 9.5 inches (24 cm) in diameter, wood-fired stoneware, photo: Will Ruggles

Pitcher, 12 inches (30 cm) in height, wood-fired stoneware, photo: Will Ruggles

Photo: Linda Harkey

A Ceramic Tradition?

Tom Turner

Last year my wife and I made our first trip to Japan, after 40 years of dreaming about it. In Japan tradition rules; here in North America we still wonder what it is. It's almost as if they are locked into tradition and we are locked out of it.

Back in the 70s, after 5 years of university art school, I was introduced to Southeastern folk pottery, and there I saw another type of tradition: I met and became friends with William J. Gordy and Lanier Meaders of Georgia; along with Dorothy and Walter Auman of North Carolina; Otto Brown of South Carolina, his brother, his son and the many Coles and Owens of North Carolina.

Tradition in Seagrove, North Carolina, or Mashiko, Japan, is about the same, just in different locations. It's based on local clays, local forms, and local customers. For a long time I have been thinking and wondering what our real American ceramic tradition is. Is it American Indian pottery; or the lead-glazed pottery of the 1700s; or the salt-glazed stoneware of the 1800s; or the alkaline glazed stoneware of the Southeastern United States in the 1800s to early 1900s? Is our real tradition from Rookwood in Cincinnati, or Weller in Zanesville?

Talking to my friend Mike Thiedeman about contemporary potters, he commented, "Our tradition is academic." I believe he's right. For many reasons, our teachers were not in touch with American traditions. Instead, they stressed the Bauhaus and Oriental pottery traditions in art school.

We threw away our traditions with the Industrial Revolution, when mass production became the norm and also the accepted way of seeing not only pottery, but all everyday items.

This, of course, was why William Morris sought to begin the Arts and Crafts Movement and why Bernard Leach carried it on, preaching in favor of the handmade. Mass production replaced the individual craftsman as glass, plastic, and refrigeration replaced the need for mainstream items in the potter's repertoire such as ceramic canning jars and liquor jugs. Store-bought butter eliminated the need for butter churns; and the mass-produced, inexpensive industrial pottery beat the potter's business to death. Fortunately for America, the Southern potters did not industrialize and as a result we still have areas like Seagrove and Jugtown as well as the Catawba Valley tradition in Vale, North Carolina. Ben Owen III in Seagrove has five generations of potting and customer education supporting his hard work today. The state of North Carolina has always supported craftsmen, and around Seagrove you can even see state highway signs pointing the way to local potters. Craft never became a dirty word there like it did in the university system. Go visit Seagrove and Jugtown, or go to Mashiko and you'll see the same thing: tradition. Japan has had about 200 generations of potters and we in North America have had about 5 or 6, but even then only in isolated areas.

We had incredible teachers back in the mid-60s. They were not potters, but they knew how to stimulate us and to direct us on our own path. We were taught not to copy and to try to find our own way. The only decent books then were by Glenn Nelson, Daniel Rhodes, and Bernard Leach. Paul Soldner had a brochure on how to build a catenary-arch kiln and Herb Sanders published a book on Japanese pottery. Richard Peeler went to Japan and made 16mm films of pottery villages, and along with Leach's book, these were the main Oriental-pottery influences in America. Then Bernard Leach traveled the world advocating the handmade pot and, in effect, he became our Pied Piper. At universities, there was a little Bauhaus and Scandinavian design thrown in, but it was Oriental pots that made the strongest impressions. Maybe Japanese brushwork related most closely to Abstract Expressionism that was then still an important movement in the New York art world. It was easy to follow Franz Kline and Jackson Pollock and Peter Voulkos, Paul Soldner, Toshiko Takaezu, and Don Reitz. They all developed dynamic brushwork on their pots. Don Frith followed more of a Scandinavian influence with his forms and surfaces, while Ralph Bacerra became the American Imari master with incredibly beautiful pots decorated in the most masterful ways. People like David Shaner developed quiet forms and decoration that was "theirs," derived from all that they could read and see around them.

In the 60s and 70s it was not the accepted route to become a potter. There were few apprenticeships available except in England and Japan. Most everyone got their MFAs and then sought or got teaching jobs. It was an exciting time to be a clay student with workshops going on all over the continent as universities developed their ceramics programs. An academic tradition was born.

The schools in their attempt to be new, different and exciting every semester, began to downplay pottery and leaned toward sculptural clay as art. Peter Voulkos, the new Pied Piper emerged at Otis Art Institute and later at Berkeley. These and other institutions filled with budding Abstract Expressionists. But the classic pot was beaten to death for the next 30 years. Since the 70s we have had a plethora of graduates coming out of schools, gaining teaching jobs, without a clue about what the art of the potter is. It's been a

big mistake. Today, I can think of only a few places where a student can work on an MFA in a pottery mode. Once in a program, students succumb to the academic pressure of making art, not craft, and they often find themselves merging into the sculptural side of clay.

It would have been smarter to allow both pots and sculpture within a ceramic art program. I know many schools today that will not allow wheelwork, or if they do, it's for one semester, before "advancing to sculptural clay." I realize, too, that many of us who really loved the art of the potter left university teaching because we wanted to make pots more than we wanted to attend meetings. People like David Shaner, Tom Coleman, Tim Mather, and Don Pilcher, to name a few of the best, got out of the university, or stopped teaching clay entirely. I left the university and felt that if I could make my very best pots, then they would be my very best teaching. Others climbed the academic ladder and became department heads, or even deans and sadly stopped making and teaching pots. Fortunately for ceramic art education Tim Mather got back into teaching and is part of a great program at Indiana University. Pilcher, now retired, is again making pots and writing. We'll all benefit from that.

It's important to point out that I am not against ceramic sculpture. Instead, I am against ceramic sculpture being touted as the art side of clay and pottery as the craft side. The trickle-down works like this: Who gets asked to jury shows and art fairs? Academics do. Since most have had no training or exposure to the art of the potter, they jury potters out and put in what looks new to them. Universities don't hire the artist with years of experience. Instead, they hire the fresh MFA graduate because their salary will be less, and they are making what is on the magazine covers. But they have little experience. Equally important, without classes on

the art of the potter, we lose not only potters, but educated customers who can appreciate really good pots.

Nevertheless, many people want to learn about pottery as well as own it and enjoy it. Art centers and private gallery/studios have sprung up out of this need for instruction. And this is not a new phenomenon. Early studios were The Torpedo Factory, 92nd Street Y in NYC, Lill St. in Chicago, and now Red Star in Kansas City along with many others. These result from a hunger for information on pottery that people can't satisfy elsewhere.

While in Japan, my wife and I visited ceramic research centers that encompass a school, a museum, and a scientific research program. All three of these divisions are entirely about clay. I wonder if it isn't time that we do the same here in North America? Perhaps it's better to just keep clay out of college and university art departments rather than try to convince them to change their ways. After all, the big difference that makes these Japanese research centers possible is that pottery is revered in Japan and often looked down upon here. While funding is the problem here in North America, perhaps we should start working on it anyway.

I know very good potters without MFAs and I've seen some very poor potters with them. I have more questions than answers, but I hope that this commentary starts a dialogue that can lead us away from where we are at present and toward a more reasonable, practical solution to educating about the art of the potter. I have been silent too long about this.

I believe we need to look critically into what is being taught as ceramic art today. Do we have a tradition? Are we too far removed at this point from our own original traditions? If the academic tradition is our substitute, is it based on anything real? Where do we go from here?

Brian Ransom

Saint Petersburg, Florida

"Whistling Water Vessel," 22 inches (56 cm) in height, vapor-fired earthenware musical instrument, water inside

"Resonating Pods VI," 34 inches (86 cm) in height, vapor-fired ceramic musical instrument

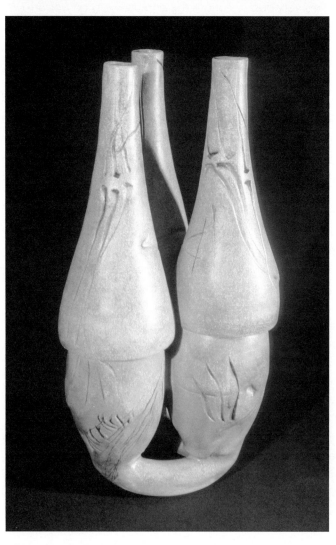

Roddy Brownlee Reed

Tampa, Florida

"Entwined," 3.75 inches (10 cm) in height, handbuilt earthenware pinch pot, brush-applied glaze and overglaze

"5,698 Spot Series, Silver Edition," 3.5 inches (9 cm) in height, handbuilt earthenware pinch pot, brush-applied glaze and overglaze including 5,698 dots

Don Reitz

Clarkdale, Arizona

"Platter #552," 22 inches (56 cm) in width,
anagama fired

Oval, Punctuated Teabowl, 3 inches (8 cm) in height, thrown and altered porcelain with "ash wind" glaze

Bowl, 9.5 inches (24 cm) in height, thrown and altered porcelain with pale blue celadon glaze

Denise Romecki

Columbus, Ohio

"A Delicate Balance," 56 inches (142 cm) in height, handbuilt stoneware and earthenware, low-fire underglaze and glaze with acrylic paint, photo: Jerry Anthony

"Keeper of the Land," 22 inches (56 cm) in height, handbuilt stoneware with Cone 5 glaze and enamel paint, photo: Jerry Anthony

Gail Russell

Lewis Center, Ohio

Copper Red Bowl, 3.5 inches (9 cm) in height, thrown porcelain, Cone 9-10 reduction, copper red glaze with iron/rutile wash and white glaze trailing, photo: Ken Van Dyne

Copper Red Casserole, 7 inches (18 cm) in height, thrown porcelain, Cone 9-10 reduction, thrown acorn finials, leaf sprigging, iron/rutile wash, photo: Ken Van Dyne

Harvey Sadow

Jupiter, Florida

"Ceramic Vessel, China Brush Series, 2003,"
11 inches (28 cm) in height, wheel-thrown stoneware,
multiple raku-fired slips and glazes,
photo: Alan Carlisle

"Ceramic Vessel, China Brush Series, 2003," 10 inches (25 cm) in height, wheel-thrown stoneware, multiple raku-fired slips and glazes, photo: Alan Carlisle

Judith Salomon

Cleveland, Ohio

Photos: A. Gray

Three Vases, 21 inches (53 cm) in height, white earthenware, slip-cast slab construction

Container, 15 inches (38 cm) in height, white earthenware, slip-cast slab construction

Brad Schwieger

Athens, Ohio

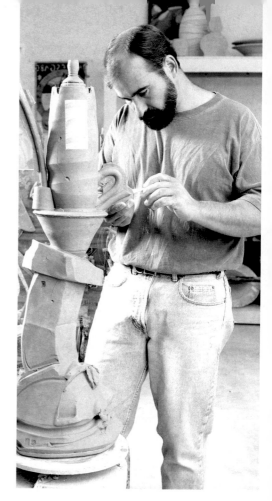

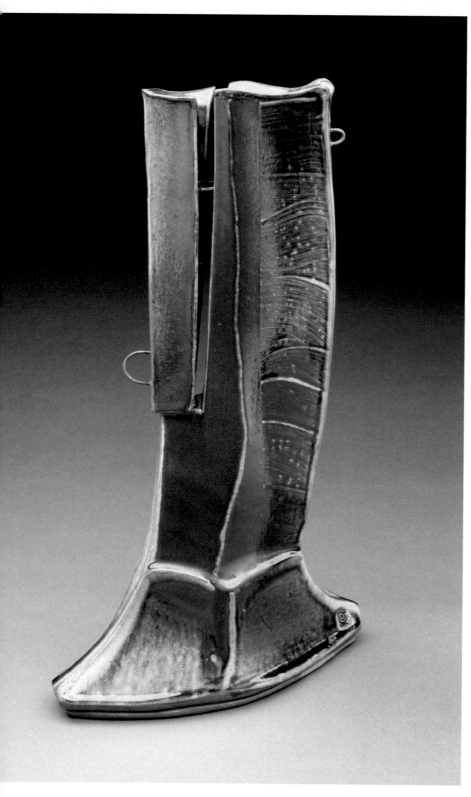

Cut Vase, 19 inches (48 cm) in height, thrown and altered stoneware, Nichrome wire, soda fired, photo: Brad Schwieger

Cut Vase, 19 inches (48 cm) in height, thrown and altered stoneware, soda fired, Cone 10, photo: Brad Schwieger

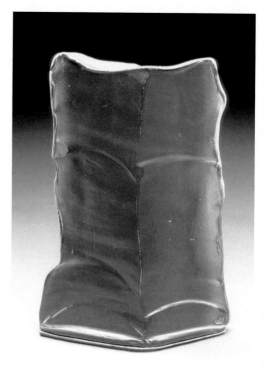

Virginia Scotchie

Columbia, South Carolina

"Pink Platter," 6 inches (15 cm) in height, handbuilt, Cone 6 oxidation-fired ceramics, photo: David Ramsey

"Two Black / Bronze Forms," 10 inches (25 cm) in height, thrown, altered, Cone 6 oxidation-fired ceramics, photo: David Ramsey

Pair, 22 inches (56 cm) in height, handbuilt terracotta with underglaze, fired to Cone 1, and wood

Storage, 20 inches (51 cm) in height, handbuilt terracotta with underglaze, fired to Cone 1, and wood

Scott Shafer

Centerville, Indiana

Bottle, 10.5 inches (27 cm) in height, slab-built stoneware, wood fired.

Box, 3.25 inches (8 cm) in height, thrown and wood-fired porcelain

Jeff Shapiro
Accord, New York

Altered Bowl with Handle, 9 inches (23 cm) in height, thrown and altered, wood fired, natural ash deposit, photo: Bob Barrett

"Encrusted Vessel," thrown, altered and wood fired, with natural ash deposit

Richard Shaw

Fairfax, California

"Clear Water," 5 inches (13 cm) in height, porcelain, cast, handbuilt, glazed with ceramic decal

"Sailboat with Dice Jar," 7.5 inches (19 cm) in height, porcelain, handbuilt, cast, glazed, underglaze, ceramic decals, photo: Joe Schoppien

"Eyes Shut," 13 inches (33 cm) in height,
Cone 6 clay and glaze fired in an electric
kiln, walnut wood

"Mouth Open," 12 inches (30 cm) in height, Cone 6 clay and glaze fired in an electric kiln,
walnut wood

Teapot, 5.5 inches (14 cm) in height, wood, oil-, and salt-fired porcelain, thrown, photo: Peter Lee

Teapot, 8.5 inches (22 cm) in height, wood-, oil-, and salt-fired porcelain, thrown, with polychrome glaze, photo: Peter Lee

"Stacked Bowls With Vase," 7 inches (18 cm) in height, thrown porcelain, refired at low temperature

"Stacked Bowls with Vase," 18 inches (46 cm) in height, thrown and altered porcelain with glaze

Michael Simon

Colbert, Georgia

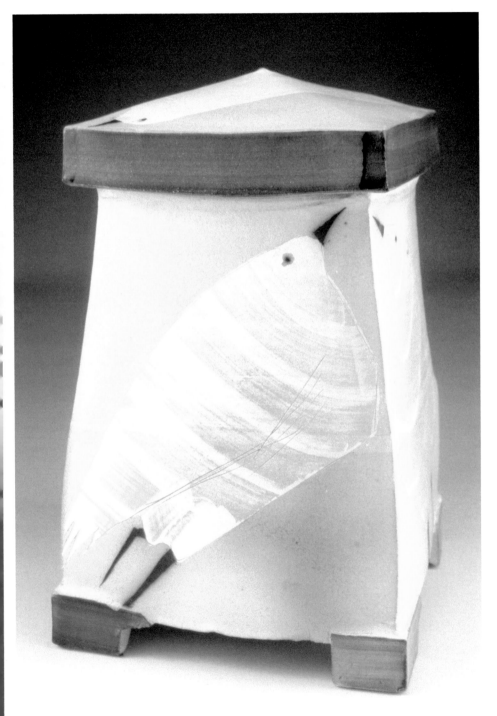

"Vase with Hole," 7 inches (18 cm) in height, salt-glazed stoneware

"Persian Jar with Bird," 14 inches (36 cm) in height, salt-glazed stoneware

Sandy Simon

Berkeley, California

"Small Covered 'Jam Jar' 2003," 5 inches (13 cm) in height, thrown porcelain, clear glaze, Nichrome wire

"Ice Cream Box," 6 inches (15 cm) in height, thrown porcelain, cut, Nichrome wire

Photos: Joe Schopplein

Mark Skudlarek

Cambridge, Wisconsin

Covered Storage Jar, 27 inches (69 cm) in height,
wood-fired stoneware with manganese slip under
ash glaze, Photo: Joe DeMaio

Jar, 13 inches (33 cm) in height, wood fired, with
natural fly ash, Photo: Joe DeMaio

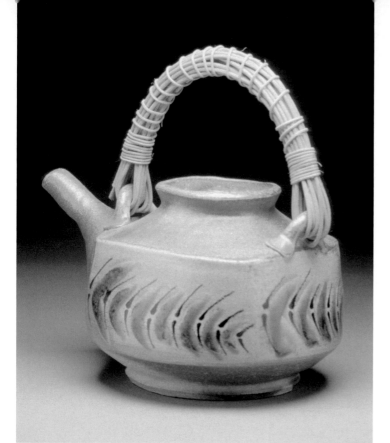

Squared Teapot, 9 inches (23 cm) in height, thrown and altered
stoneware, slip glaze decorated, soda fired, photo: McKenzie Smith

Platter, 20 inches (51 cm) in height, thrown stoneware, slip-glaze decorated, soda fired, photo: McKenzie Smith

Nan Smith

Gainesville, Florida

"Reaching," 21.5 inches (55 cm) in height, sculpted and press molded, glazed earthenware with airbrushed underglaze, mounted on Plexiglas

"Clarity," 27.5 inches (70 cm) in height, sculpted and press molded, glazed earthenware with airbrushed underglaze, laminated wood pedestal

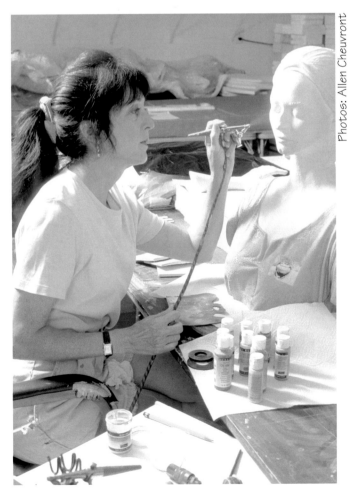

Photos: Allen Cheuvront

Jaqueline Cohen & Vaughn Smith

High Falls, New York

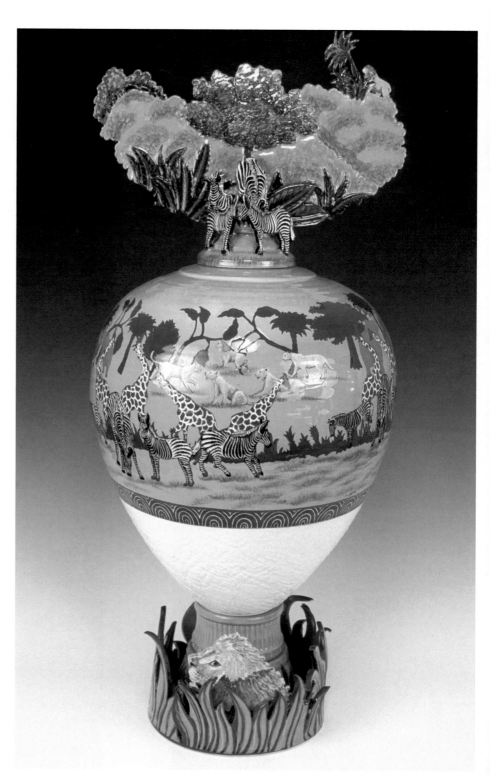

"Pecking Order," 22 inches (56 cm) in height, thrown earthenware, painted and stenciled with slips and underglazes, with
handbuilding on lid

"African Sundown," 30 inches (76 cm) in height,
thrown white stoneware with painted, stenciled and
carved slip decoration, slab building on base and lid

Cricket Cage, 6 inches (15 cm) in height, thrown and constructed glazed stoneware, fired to Cone 10

Jar, 8 inches (20 cm) in height, thrown and slab-built, underglazed clay, saggar fired to Cone 06

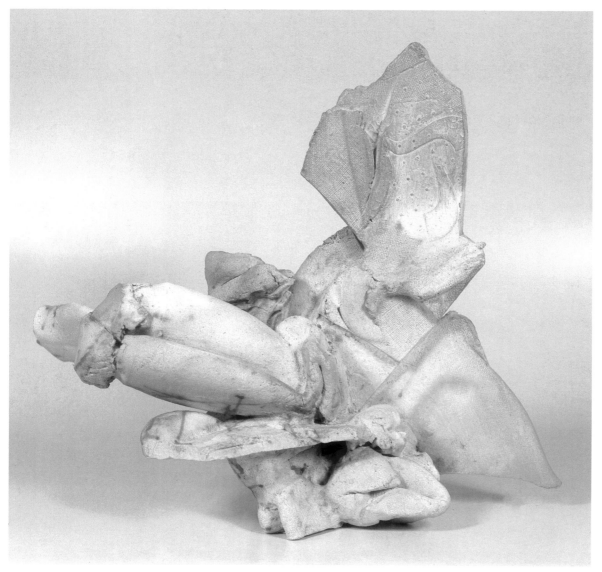

"Tea Bowl with Tea Box 03-04," 5 inches (13 cm) in height, thrown and altered clay, unglazed, high-temperature wood fired, photo: Paul Soldner

"Sculpture 03-05," 26.5 inches (67 cm) in height, thrown and altered clay, off-wheel built, with slips, Cone 5 salt glazed, photo: Paul Soldner

"Tool Box," 14 inches (36 cm) in height, whiteware, with glaze and luster

"Paint Tray," 9 inches (23 cm) in height, whiteware with low-fire glaze and luster

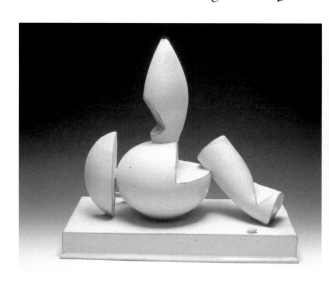

Chris Staley

State College, Pennsylvania

"Still Life," 10 inches (25 cm) in height, thrown and handbuilt, salt-glazed stoneware

Teapot and 2 Cups, 8 inches (20 cm) in height, thrown, salt-glazed stoneware

Irma Starr

Kansas City, Missouri

Photo: Irma Starr

"Commemorative Dish 21st Century Ceramics: Sculpture," 18 inches (46 cm) in diameter, thrown earthenware, decoration in the style of 17th-century English slipware

"Commemorative Dish for 21st Century Ceramics: Pottery," 18 inches (46 cm) in diameter, thrown earthenware, decoration in the style of 17th-century English slipware

John Stephenson

Ann Arbor, Michigan

"Mariner's Tool #14," 14 inches (36 cm) in height, handbuilt terracotta,
photo: John Stephenson

"Undertow #2," 19 inches (48 cm) in height, handbuilt terracotta with white slip surface, photo: John Stephenson

The Functional Pot

Val Cushing

Although the situation is improving somewhat, the functional (utilitarian) pot, a vital part of contemporary ceramics, does not often get the recognition and visibility it deserves. The gradual emergence of the "vessel" and ceramic sculpture, and their dominance over pottery in exhibitions and in the media has created an odd and misleading situation. Misleading, because most people who make their living in the studio are functional potters. When it comes to selling enough work to be self-supporting, very few can do it by making vessels and sculpture. Yet the best work of this large group of potters is under-represented in the public's eye.

I have seen many exhibitions and juried some, all over America and in other parts of the world. Frequently I travel, lecture, give workshops, visit museums and galleries, look at many of the books and magazines in our field and, generally, keep informed about ceramic art. What impresses and worries me as a result is how invisible the functional potter tends to be in the media, in schools and in galleries and museums. Why is this so?

Part of the reason, and the problem, begins in art schools where ceramics is frequently presented to

students as a study of vessels and sculpture. Pottery is either not taught, or the students are discouraged from that path. In these schools (and art school is where most ceramists get started), functional pottery making is thought of as only a craft. Further, function-less clay objects are presented as more pertinent to art studies. This is, of course, an old and tiresome argument that exists mainly in the Western art world and among various other "taste makers." But, isn't art really about asking questions, about problem-solving and developing concepts and ideas about visual experience? Functional-pottery making is an ideal vehicle for that sort of study. Beauty and innovation does also exist in pottery. It is not exclusive to vessels and sculpture. The useful pot sends a clear message that the humanizing values of art and function are alive and well. It communicates to people. It helps one to know and understand that art objects can be seen as ennobling and personalizing rather than alienating as so many art shows now seem to be. There are special and wonderful qualities to be found in functional pottery; the kinds of things that writer Margaret Visser (talking about staple foods) called "sublime in the ordinary." Pottery in use becomes part of our lives in special ways. The art world and many artists have become more and more apart from the world around them.

With pottery, I sometimes feel

that what isn't spoken is what you listen for. The sensuous qualities of pottery are part of what suggests that thought, especially touch, but not touch alone. Whereas painting and sculpture are mainly about seeing and the brain, pottery engages all the senses. Sensuality does have something to do with time and contemplation and with real experience. In these ways pottery can help us meet our psychological as well as our visual needs. A pot can generate emotional power in many ways but the impact is often found in the subtleties, the implications and the nuances. Considering how this information is interpreted through the senses, it makes one realize that the message of functional pottery, whether on the conscious or subliminal level, might go far beyond simple use.

As I said, things are getting better. We do have occasional exhibitions and a conference or two that focuses on functional pottery. A few individual potters have received deserved recognition and magazines, such as *Ceramics Monthly* and *Studio Potter*, have given equal time to potters and to the functional pot. It may be asking too much to hope that the bias against pottery that exists in the art world and elsewhere would finally be overcome, the way other biases and prejudices in our society are fading. As long as beauty has relevance, pottery will be important to humanity.

"Yellow Beach," 27 inches (69 cm) in height, thrown and handbuilt terracotta vase with colored slips, some mixed with paper and vitreous slips in the cracks

Photos: John Stephenson

"Yellow Wave," 24 inches (61 cm) in height, thrown and handbuilt terracotta wall plate with colored slips and vitreous slips

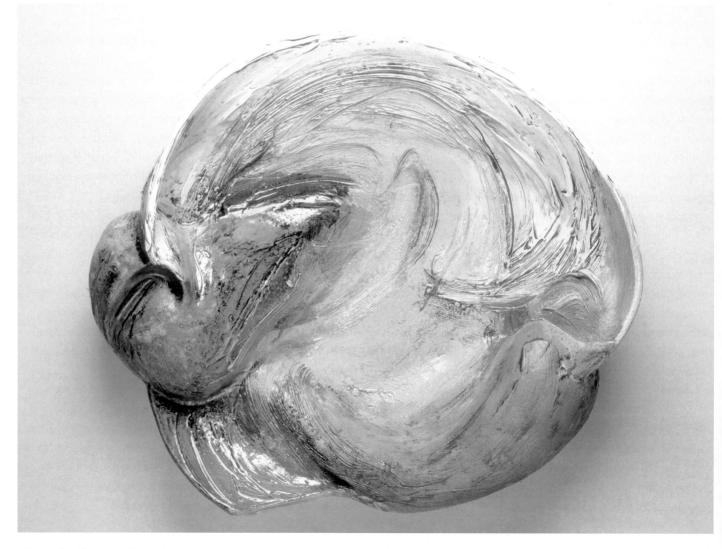

Jacquie Stevens

Santa Fe, New Mexico

Vessel, handbuilt earthenware
with raised slip decoration

Vessel, handbuilt and pierced
earthenware with woven fiber

Photo: Toshi Otsuki

"Angelo Da Venocemmia," 13 inches (33 cm) in height, slab constructed porcelain painted with underglazes and oxides, photo: John Polak

"Bella Toscana, 2002," 22 inches (56 cm) in height, porcelain relief painted with underglazes and oxides, photo: John Polak

Kaname Takada

Columbus, Ohio

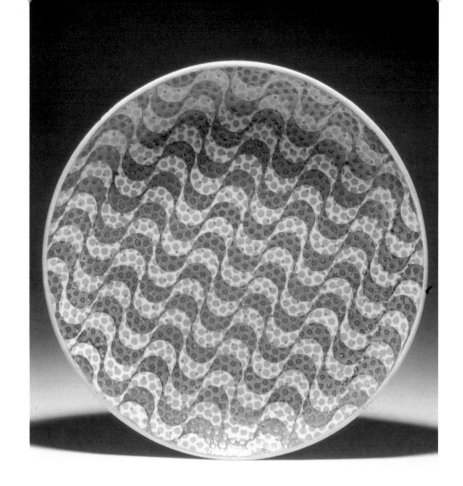

"Bowl, 2003-03," 21.5 inches (55 cm) in diameter, wheel-thrown red earthenware, colored slip and glaze, oxidation fired to Cone 4

"Bowl, 2003-02," 21.25 inches (54 cm) in diameter, wheel-thrown red earthenware, colored slip and glaze, oxidation fired to Cone 4

"Untitled," 16 inches (41 cm) in height, glazed stoneware

"Untitled," 9 inches (23 cm) in height, glazed stoneware

The Future of Pots

Scott Cooper

Perhaps the greatest thing about 21st century ceramics is that there is still abundant room for handmade utilitarian pots. I doubt that many observers could have predicted this a hundred years ago. At the turn of the last century, all the trends were heading in the opposite direction.

In 1903, most rural American potteries had yet to die out. But they would, and the signs were already there: concerns for safety and sanitation, a rising middle class with finer tastes, inklings of not only mass-produced pots, but mass tastes and aesthetics as well. From an historical perspective, handmade pots looked doomed.

How could we have anticipated the successive waves of change that led to where we are now? These include influence from the Arts & Crafts movement, the revolutions by Voulkos, Arneson and others, the rise of a place for clay in academia and the subsequent pluralism of the last twenty years. None of these followed a predictable path. One could argue that, against that background, utilitarian pots never went away. They just faded in and out of prominence. But to me, the fact that they're still here at all is something of a marvel.

When I first heard the title for this book, I couldn't help but think of superconductors and nose cones, high-tech insulators and robotic mass-casting operations; and this from a potter who uses a treadle wheel! What must the general public think when it comes to that confusing intersection of clay and the next hundred years? And why are those space-age thoughts still my instinctual reaction to the idea of the future?

No one on Star Trek ever drank from a handmade mug. Not that I was watching all that closely, but the inherent message was that the future held no room for such quaint artifacts as crafts. The only pots I saw in Star Wars were on the grubby, backwards desert planet of Tatooine where, presumably, Luke Skywalker's family couldn't afford the latest in chrome and plastic tableware. And while it would be silly to expect or allow these film versions of the future to predict the current state of ceramic art, they and countless others certainly informed my childhood expectations. Little did I know, as I started down the path to being a potter, that those subconscious lessons had lingered into adulthood.

When I started making pots in 1990, I had a sense that I was getting in on the tail end of something; that the millenium, or something like it, would signal an end to this quaintly archaic process of shaping clay by hand. As my interest evolved into commitment (and then to something of an obsession), I feared that a tipping point was coming that would make it all for naught; that this area of artistic inquiry had a lifespan, a shelf-life, and I'd arrived on the scene too late. This was a naive fear, to be sure, and fairly self-indulgent at that, but it held a grain of truth. For example, while traditional wet photography is certainly not dead, the astounding changes brought by the emergence of digital photography over the last few years demonstrate the effects that advancing technology can wreak on traditional artistic processes. My fears were not that far misplaced.

But I gradually realized that there would be no Y2K for clay. If anything, the new century would be better for ceramic art than the last. I once asked Clary Illian about cycles and trends: her reply was that, for 30 years, each one had been better than the last. I believe that the more time we spend in front of computer monitors and TV screens, the more virtual life gets, the greater the interest in tangible, handmade, one-of-a-kind objects.

I find it hard to imagine the status of our field a hundred years ago, before the ceramists of the 20th century became the newest layer of a foundation for us to build on, "standing on the shoulders of giants," indeed. I envision better pots, better sculpture, better kilns, better glazes, better customers, better galleries, better shows, better schools, better artists. But also more competition, more self-promotion, more technology, more blurring of intent, more highly evolved niches, more splitting of finer and finer hairs.

This future is where I will spend the bulk of my career. If I make a contribution, it is forthcoming in those hazy times. If my chosen strain of ceramics goes out of fashion, I'll become retro. If pots should happen to move to the top of the clay family heap for a while, I'll go along in tow. Whatever comes, it's going to be mighty interesting.

"The World is at Your Fingertips, 2003," 38 inches (97 cm) in height, thrown and altered stoneware, fired to Cone 3 in reduction, with terra sigillata surfacing, photo: Michael Watson

"Open Mandala with Iron Spike, 2003," 37 inches (94 cm) in height, thrown and altered stoneware, fired to Cone 3 in reduction, with terra sigillata surfacing, photo: Michael Watson

Faceted Jar, 8.5 inches (22 cm) in height, thrown and faceted stoneware

Lidded Bowl, 5.25 inches (13 cm) in height, thrown and faceted stoneware

Brother Thomas

Erie, Pennsylvania

"Small Vase, Honan Temmoku," 10.75 inches (27 cm) in height, thrown and glazed clay, photo: Max Coniglio

Photo: Bill Aron

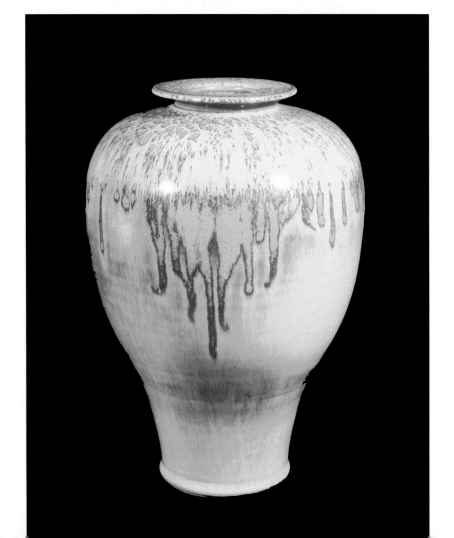

"Vase, Mei P'ing Form," 12.5 inches (32 cm) in height, thrown clay with iron yellow and kaki glaze

Steven Thurston

Columbus, Ohio

"Boullee's Bubbles No 2," 70 inches (178 cm) in height, castable refractory with poplar and miscellaneous hardware, photo: Steven Thurston

"Composition No. 6: Equality," 72 inches (183 cm) in height, castable refractory with poplar and miscellaneous hardware

Photo: Allen Cheuvront

John Tilton

Alachua, Florida

Round Jar, 9 inches (23 cm) in height, thrown porcelain with crystalline glaze, photo: John Tilton

Round Jar, 9 inches (23 cm) in height, thrown porcelain with multi-fired matt crystalline glaze, photo: John Tilton

Dorothy Torivivio

Acoma, New Mexico

Vessel, handbuilt earthenware with geometric slip decoration

Vessel, handbuilt earthenware with geometric slip decoration

Whittling Away the Middleman

Todd Piker

"Decorative Arts" has become the catchall phrase to redefine the efforts of people engaged in creating objects made of clay. This nomenclature began in the mid-1980s. Cheap imports have rendered the American potter obsolete; once and for all if we're not careful. There was a pronounced shift in American art schools. A determined effort was made to dissuade interest in production pots. Clay students were urged to embrace the creation of "objects." It is a familiar tale written by market forces. Out of the gate, a mug is simply not worth as much as a vessel. These new clay artists, who are supposed to make statements, are now lined up like racehorses with their pedigrees from gallery stables. So we are decorative artists. The job description for "potter" has ceased to exist. Those of us that insist on working in clay will have to measure up to standards being developed by leaders in this new field. For a current list of these arbiters of taste pick up the latest catalogue of SOFA (the Sculptural Object and Functional Art show). It is a grim reminder of the current trend to see how few purveyors of functional art there are in comparison to those promoting sculptural objects in this venue. The more one tries to ignore this reality, the harder it will be to make a living as a potter. But there is a faint glimmer of hope.

In North Carolina the public has chosen to bypass the generally usurious distribution system that exists elsewhere. In my 30 years as a potter I have neither seen nor heard of so many pots sold at kiln openings as are sold by potters in North Carolina. This stands out as a testament to the good sense of the makers and buyers in that state. Will Ruggles and Douglass Rankin can even find a way to get the public across impossible terrain to line up and buy their pots. Surely part of the magic is in their years of diligent hard work and effort. They make great pots and are sensitive to the direct link they have with their public. But it is also a clarion call signaling the efficiency of a marketplace that brings the buyer right to the kiln door. There are significant efficiencies to be realized in this kind of business economics and we all should take a page from that book.

The 21st century will be about whittling away at the middlemen in all economic exchanges. The Internet has started this process and for potters it can become our doorway to a future that will connect us with people that still understand the value of functional vessels. Surely there will always be settings such as the one at Columbus College of Art and Design that sparked this book, and Phyllis Blair Clark's wonderful Functional Ceramics Workshops. In both these venues, pots can be compared and critiqued on their merits. But we must not allow the institutions (particularly the university/gallery cartels) to dictate our sensibilities. In the words of my esteemed colleague John Leach, "Potters of the world, ignite!"

Jack Troy

Huntingdon, Pennsylvania

Porcelain Bowl, 16 inches (41 cm) in diameter, thrown and anagama fired, photo: Paul Hazi

Covered Jar, 16 inches (41 cm) in height, thrown stoneware and anagama fired, photo: Paul Hazi

Ann Tubbs

Ottawa Lake, Michigan

"The Juggler," 14 inches (36 cm) in
width, slab-built clay with twisted
handles, Cone 2-3 majolica glaze under
polychrome colorants, photo: Jerry
Anthony

"The Devil and Ms. Majolica," 15 inches (38 cm) in height,
slab-built clay with slip and additions of majolica glaze,
post-bisque carbonizing (smoked cold) and acrylic paint,
photo: Jerry Anthony

Photos: Ken Van Dyne

"Large Carved Jar with Bird Sentinels," 16 inches (41 cm) in height, thrown porcelain, honey ash glaze, green and white glaze dots, reduction fired to Cone 9

"Bird Vase," 8 inches (20 cm) in height, thrown porcelain, paddled, carved, blue teadust and flambé glazes with iron, reduction fired to Cone 9

"Iron Spot Covered Urn," 13 inches (33 cm) in height, wheel-thrown, wood-fired stoneware

Covered Jar, 6.5 inches (17 cm) in height, wheel-thrown, wood-fired stoneware

Triesch Voelker

Corrales, New Mexico

Oil Jar, 8 inches (20 cm) in height, thrown, soda-fired stoneware

Stacking Canister/Food Server, 9 inches (23 cm) in height, thrown, soda-fired stoneware

Patti Warashina

Seattle, Washington

LEFT: "Storm Warning," 37.5 inches (95 cm) in height, whiteware with underglaze and glaze with steel stand, photo: Rob Vinnedge

RIGHT: "Silent Breeze," 41 inches (104 cm) in height, earthenware with underglaze, glaze and aluminum with steel stand, photo: Rob Vinnedge

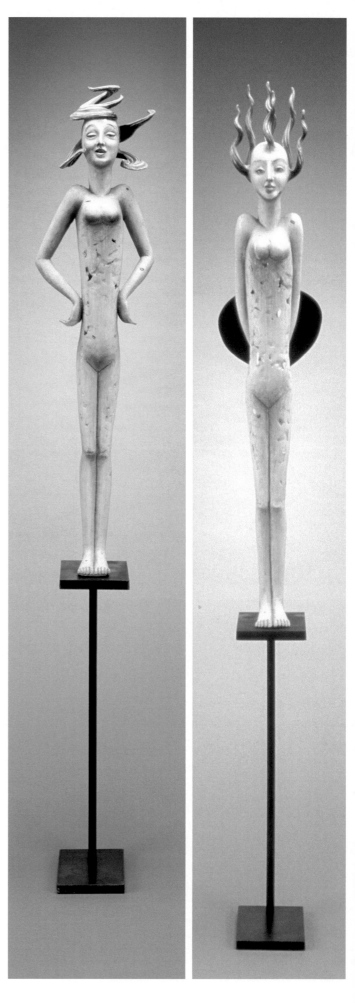

"Guardian," 9 inches (23 cm) in height, thrown and handbuilt raku, double-wall form, photo: Hershel Womack

Photo: Sarah Waters

"Guardian," 9 inches (23 cm) in height, thrown, handbuilt and fumed double-wall form, photo: Hershel Womack

Kurt Weiser

Tempe, Arizona

"Caucasian," 16.5 inches (42 cm) in height, porcelain with overglaze enamel; courtesy of Garth Clark Gallery, NYC

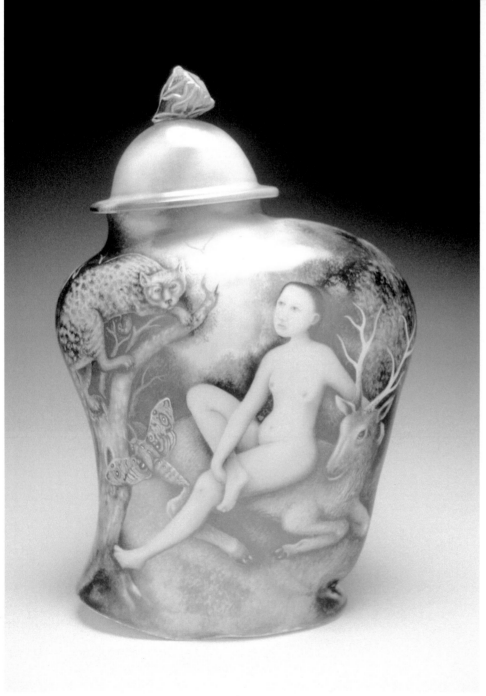

"Progress Report," 28 inches (71 cm) in height, Cone 1 terracotta, Cone 04 glaze, photo: R. R. Jones

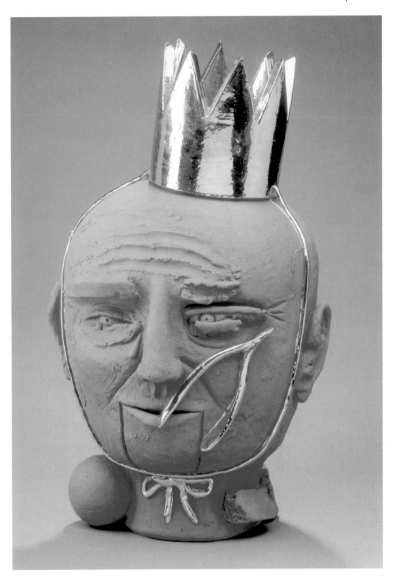

"Worried Man," 27 inches (69 cm) in height, Cone 1 terracotta, Cone 018 gold luster, photo: R. R. Jones

Photo: Ellie Brown

Tom White

Northfield, Massachusetts

Coffee Server with Mugs, 10 inches (25 cm) in height, wheel-thrown stoneware, Shino glaze with crackle slip, reduction fired to Cone 11, photo: John Polak

Teapot with Cups, 7 inches (18 cm) in width, wheel-thrown stoneware, Shino glaze with crackle slip, reduction fired to Cone 11, photo: John Polak

Gerry Williams

Dunbarton, New Hampshire

"Inside/Outside Form #1," 23.5 inches (60 cm) in height, thrown and applied stoneware with ash glaze, photo: Gerry Williams

"Inside/Outside Form #2," 22 inches (56 cm) in height, thrown and applied stoneware with ash glaze, photo: Gerry Williams

Bob Winokur

Horsham, Pennsylvania

"The Other Side of the House 2001," 11 inches (28 cm) in height, constructed in three parts of brick-clay slabs and salt fired to Cone 9-10 in reduction

"The House As A Pedestal 2002," 19.5 inches (50 cm) in height, constructed of brick-clay slabs and salt fired to Cone 9-10 in reduction

Photo: Paula Winokur

Photo: Robert Winokur

Paula Winokur

Horsham, Pennsylvania

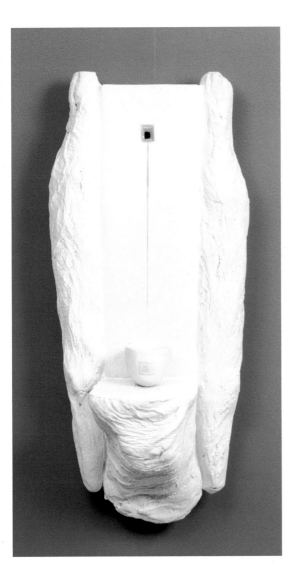

"Shrine for a Small Bowl," 26 inches (66 cm) in height, slab-constructed porcelain, thrown bowl, with ceramic pencil, sulfates, and chlorides, photo: John Carlano

"Repetition I 2002," 16 inches (41 cm) in height, handbuilt porcelain, thrown bowls (glazed interiors), with ceramic pencil, sulfates and chlorides, photo: John Carlano

"Day of the Dead (Dia de los Muertes)," 18 inches (46 cm) in height, thrown and handbuilt stoneware wall piece

"The Dance of Good & Evil (Danza del Bien y del Mal)," 28 inches (71 cm) in height, thrown and handbuilt stoneware vessel

"Wall Piece #1," 6 inches (15 cm) in height, stoneware, slab-thrown rim, wood ash glaze

"Wall Piece #2," 5 inches (13 cm) in height, stoneware, slab-thrown rim, wood ash glaze

Malcolm Wright

Marlboro, Vermont

Vase, 13 inches (33 cm) in height, thrown, wood-fired stoneware with Shino glaze, photo: John Polak

Platter, 2.5 inches (6 cm) in height, thrown, wood-fired brick clay, photo: John Polak

Majolica Begging Bowl, 12 inches (30 cm) in width,
Tin-glazed terracotta with polychrome overglaze
decoration and gold luster

Majolica Plate, 10.5 inches (27 cm) in width,
Tin-glazed terracotta with polychrome overglaze
decoration and gold luster

Photos: Josh DeWeese

Canadian Clay, eh!

By Robin Hopper

Ceramics is almost certainly the most eclectic of visual art disciplines; it mixes and matches almost everything from the aesthetics of the Orient to the technology of Tupperware and sometimes even the aesthetics of Tupperware with the technology of the Orient! With a many-thousand year history, styles and processes of the ceramic past have always been the launch pad for the ceramic future. Since most globally-aware contemporary ceramic artists extract freely from the same plethora of historical objects and images of historical objects, the likelihood of anything truly original in clay is questionable. No matter how diverse, drawing from the same sources inevitably brings about similar visualizations, and what delineates American contemporary clay works from Australian, British, Danish, Canadian or any other culture, I think lies more in the nature of the maker than their country of origin. To state that any one person can be viewed as the quintessential example of what their country of birth should produce fails to consider the background and influences of the individual. The United States' most acclaimed ceramic artist of the last century was Peter Voulkos, a man of Greek origins probably with intuitive Greek values of proportion,

form, content and surface. Is his work truly American or a synthesis of multi-cultural sources heavily influenced by Greek ancestry? How much is intuitive and how much a result of extraneous sensual bombardment?

If Voulkos can be regarded as the prime representative of American ceramics, is there such a thing as a "Canadian Clay" identity? Although there is no work by Voulkos in it, viewers of this important bi-national exhibition and readers of this book will have to judge for themselves. I believe that there is, although it is difficult to say why and almost impossible to categorically assess just what delineates that cultural identity, bombarded as we all are by works and wares from the farthest reaches of the globe. As a generality, and generalities are always dangerous ground, I find that Canadians as a multicultural community are quieter, less violent, more conservative, less bombastic, more tolerant, more environmentally conscious and more aware of the whole world and its diversity of cultures than our neighbors to the south. I think that these differences in group personality and our perception of the world greatly inform both the people and the work that is done here. In general, I find Canadian clay to be

quite representative of this country and its people: quiet, unassuming, thoughtful, and exploratory with great strength of commitment and deep integrity. As a transplanted Brit, living and working in Canada for the last 35 years and traveling widely around the world both studying and teaching, I have been fortunate to observe the "world ceramic scene" from many vantage points. As a writer of books on ceramic subject matter, I solicit images from artists around the world and am currently in correspondence with several hundred potters and ceramic artists. I try to keep my eyes and mind open.

The exhibition, on which this book is based, contains work by approximately 250 of the most acclaimed and visible of North American contemporary ceramic artists. The fact that almost 20 percent are from Canada suggests that clay is alive and well north of the border, but only time will tell if there is such a thing as a unique Canadian perspective and where we might fit. I personally prefer to think that as we are all individuals with wildly differing life journeys to where we are now, our work should somehow reflect that journey. If the journey reflects the country of origin it will come through in the work produced.

Robert Archambeau

Winnipeg, Manitoba

Pair of Teapots, 8 inches (20 cm) in height, wood fired to Cone 12, reglazed, then wood fired again in soda kiln to Cone 10, photo: Jeff Burke

Fluted Vase, 13 inches (33 cm) in height, crackle slip under amber glaze, wood fired to Cone 12,
photo: Jeff Burke

John Chalke

Calgary, Alberta

Pitcher with Integrated Handle, 9.25 inches (23 cm) in height, soda-vapor-glazed stoneware

Photos: Barbara Tipton

Pitcher with Integrated Handle, 11 inches (28 cm) in height, soda-vapor-glazed stoneware

(Detail) "To Be... #1," 5.7 inches (14 cm) in height, handbuilt Cone 6 paper clay, multifired from Cone 6 to Cone 06 in oxidation, with Styrofoam tray and Plexiglas, photo: Ying-Yueh Chuang

"Plant Creature #8," 5.5 inches (14 cm) in height, handbuilt Cone 6 paper clay, multifired from Cone 6 to Cone 06 in oxidation, photo: Ying-Yueh Chuang

Bruce Cochrane

Mississauga, Ontario

Cruet Set, 10 inches (25 cm) in height, thrown and
wood-fired porcelain with stoneware slab

Photos: Peter Hogan

Stacked Containers, 14 inches (36 cm) in height,
press-molded with thrown elements, salt-glazed to
Cone 10 with stoneware slab

Karen Dahl

Winnipeg, Manitoba

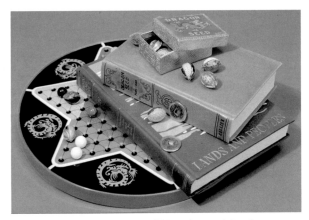

"Dragon Seed," 12.5 inches (32 cm) in width, slip-cast and handbuilt earthenware with glazes, underglazes and luster

"Spilt Ink," 12 inches (30 cm) in width, slip-cast and handbuilt earthenware with glazes, underglazes and luster

Walter Dexter

Victoria, British Columbia

"Falling Light," 20 inches (51 cm) in height, stoneware, fired to Cone 6 in oxidation, then fired down to Cone 05

"Darkness Before Light," 19.5 inches (50 cm) in height, stoneware, fired to Cone 6 in oxidation, then fired down to Cone 05

Judi Dyelle

Victoria, British Columbia

"Contemplation Bowl — Kamloops Series," 13 inches (33 cm) in diameter, thrown porcelain, fired to Cone 10 in reduction, photo: Tony Starck

"Pierced Bowl – Crystal Pink Series," 10.66 inches (27 cm) in diameter, thrown porcelain, fired to Cone 10 in reduction, photo: Tony Starck

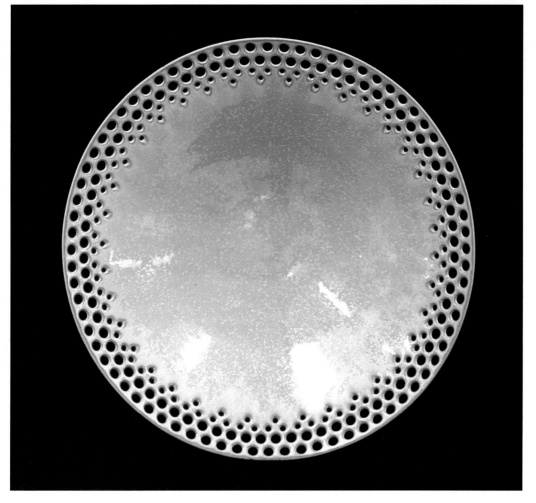

Neil Forrest

Glen Margaret, Nova Scotia

"Trivet: Barge," 17 inches (43 cm) in width, fired whiteware, photo: Steve Farmer

"Lung of Istanbul," 19 inches (48 cm) in height, fritted porcelain with metal pins and vinyl tubing, photo: Neil Forrest

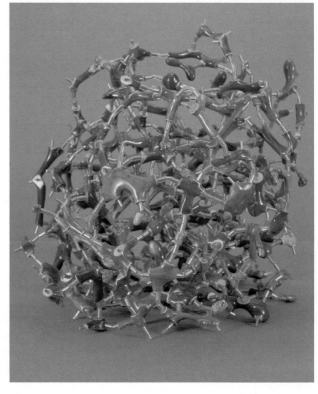

Leopold L. Foulem

Montreal, Quebec

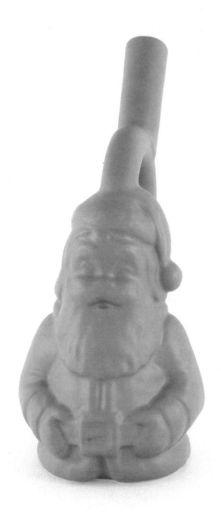

"Imari-Style Teapot in Mounts," 10 inches (25 cm) in height, slab-built low-fire earthenware with decals, gold luster, and found objects

"Santa Claus Head Vessel with Stirrup Spout," 12.75 inches (32 cm) in height, press-molded low-fire earthenware

Steven Heinemann

Richmond Hill, Ontario

"Untitled (Blue Disc)," 22 inches (56 cm) in height, cast earthenware, multiple firings, photo: Steven Heinemann

"Untitled (Large Disc)," 31 inches (79 cm) in height, cast earthenware, multiple firings, photo: Steven Heinemann

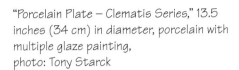

Robin Hopper

Victoria, British Columbia

"Porcelain Plate – Clematis Series," 13.5 inches (34 cm) in diameter, porcelain with multiple glaze painting,
photo: Tony Starck

"Feather Basket Plate," 13 inches (33 cm) in diameter, tri-colored agate porcelain, photo: Tony Starck

Harlan House

Marysville, Ontario

Photo: R. W. House

"Mei P'ing," 13.25 inches (34 cm) in height, thrown porcelain with slip and glaze, including celadons

Tulip Vase, 5.8 inches (15 cm) in height, thrown and reeded porcelain with celadon glaze

Gordon Hutchens

Denman Island, British Columbia

Pot with Handle, 12.5 inches (32 cm) in height, thrown stoneware, pulled handle, anagama fired to Cone 12, natural ash glaze

Plate, 11 inches (28 cm) in diameter, porcelain with slip glaze, fired to Cone 10, refired low for gold and metallic salts

Denys James

Saltspring Island, British Columbia

"Floating," 13 inches (33 cm) in height, terracotta wall relief fired to Cone 5 with slips and stains, photo: Denys James

"Waiting," 13 inches (33 cm) in height, terracotta fired to Cone 5 with slip and stain decoration, photo: Denys James

Cathi Jefferson

North Vancouver, British Columbia

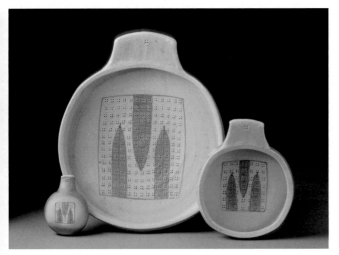

Photos: John Sinal

3 Leaf Strainers, the largest is 14 inches (36 cm) in width, wheel-thrown and altered stoneware, salt/soda-fired

3 Gravy Boats, the largest is 7 inches (18 cm) in height, wheel-thrown and altered stoneware, salt/soda-fired

Enid Legros-Wise

Paspebiac, Quebec

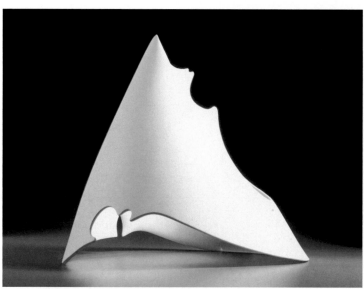

"Patriot Portrait...we are in our cups...
The child's cup of wonder...
The student's cup of learning...
The Adventurer's cup of quest...
The soldier's cup of courage...
The statesman's cup of peaceful solutions...
The achiever's cup of steadfast dreams...
The liberator's cup of renewed hope...
The seeker's cup of spirit...
The philosopher's cups of sorrow, silence and song...
The patriot's cup of trust...,"
the largest 7.5 inches (19 cm) in height, cast, carved,
reduction-fired bisque porcelain; stands for the cups are
hand-formed, unglazed raku, photo: Enid Legros-Wise

"Wave Sculpture 4-59," 8.125 inches (21 cm) in height, slab-molded
and carved low-fire paper clay, paint, photo: Enid Legros-Wise

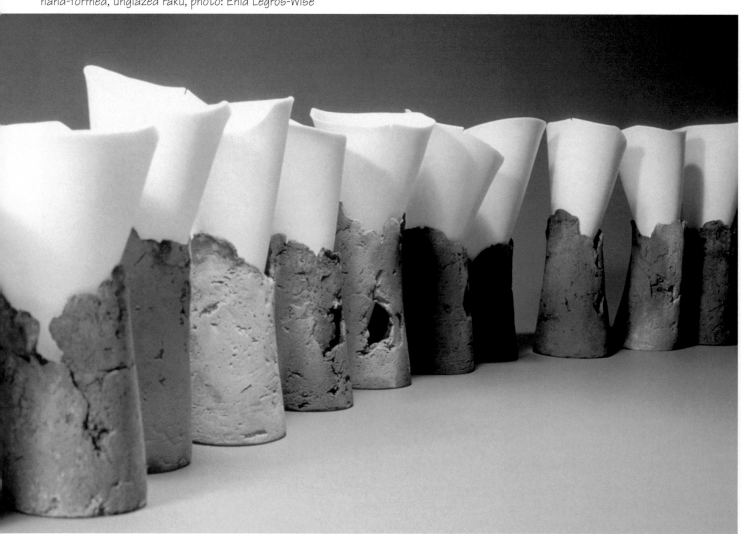

Photo: R. W. Sandford

Les Manning

Medicine Hat, Alberta

"Wind-Swept," 11.5 inches (29 cm) in height, thrown and altered laminated stoneware and porcelain with post-fire sandblasted surface, photo: Kevin Dykstra

"Glacial Flow," 5.75 inches (15 cm) in height, thrown and altered laminated stoneware and porcelain with post-fire sandblasted surface, photo: Kevin Dykstra

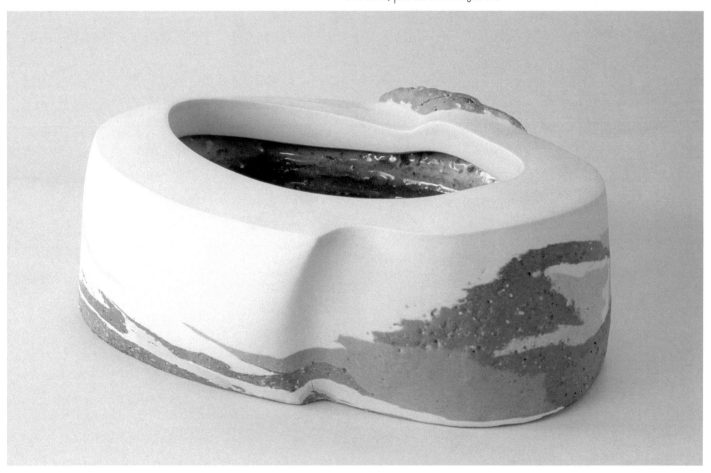

Paul Mathieu

Vancouver, British Columbia

FAR LEFT: "J.K. 86-82 (From Sculpture Series), Salt and Pepper Shakers," 7 inches (18 cm) in height, cast, glazed and lustered porcelain from an edition of 5

"W.T.C., 9-11-01 (From Disasters Series) Salt and Pepper Shakers," 7 inches (18 cm) in height, cast, glazed and lustered porcelain from an edition of 5

Photo: Richard Harrison

Richard Milette

Montreal, Quebec

Photos: Pierre Gauvin

"Teapot N 6491," 6.66 inches (17 cm) in height, thrown and handbuilt white earthenware with glazes, gold luster and decals

"Garniture with Pink Ground and Rebuses," 10.5 inches (27 cm) in height, thrown white earthenware with glazes and enamels

What's Ahead for Ceramics in the 21st century?

Karen Thuesen Massaro

What's coming in this still-new century? Years of solo work in the studio do not make me overly confident about what I see in my porcelain ball, but it looks like diversity and fluidity will continue to shape our art. What does that mean? We are so fortunate in North America to have the right to freedom of expression. When we follow it, what we want to pursue at first changes, then comes around almost full circle, and splits into myriad directions.

This may sound odd, but in some ways it doesn't matter what our ceramics look like: tall, short, royal blue, sky blue, turquoise. When I'm painting a piece, the color choice can seem like a very big deal; but really, what does it matter? We follow our noses not knowing what ideas will be of interest now or in the future. What is essential is that we create a studio experience where we are confident in following a current interest: working on the next Shino teabowl; political sculpture concerning current events; erotica; representational mice; abstract machine parts; process oriented, preplanned, robotically formed, painted, glazed, dreamscapes. There are lots of things worth caring about.

The art world is fragile and usually the first sector to be affected by an economic downturn. The gallery system treads water as it casts for diminishing collectors. We all find ways of waiting for better times. Studio potters continue to pursue the goal of making objects for people to live with rather than next to.

The potter's work benefits from years of skill-building, and there is the persistent challenge of connecting with customers who appreciate your work enough to buy it. In my experience, selling pots in galleries can present a difficulty. In this context, the vessel becomes too expensive for the consumer and generates too little income for both the potter and the gallery. So potters learn to nourish business relationships directly with their customers. This, of course, is also a challenge. Websites offer another connection between independent potters and their admirers or consumers of their work. This works particularly well for a shy potter living in a rural setting. I just hope the purchased pots can become the ultimate installations enabling life's experiences. That's where they shine.

Movement of peoples leads to cultural diversity. Ideas can be shared by many professions. We have obvious affinities to other art forms. Major discoveries in science and technology will continue to shape how we think and practice our craft. Now we have desktop personal computers and they have become fabrication tools as well. It won't be long before personal robots come to the studio. Will we use these tools for artistic inquiry or will we become manufacturers? Perhaps we will divide the road again and do both.

Private lives affect public work. Navigating our personal lives to include professional goals will remain one of life's challenges. Fortunately, in my lifetime, we have come to accept the varied nature of personal choices. A woman can have a child while young and be a good mother without fear of losing her brain cells by firing only toast for 15 years. She can stay with clay or just let it rest for a while. She is also free not to have children and can expect a long life with love and warm friendships, plus a lot more time to work. Lifestyle is a matter of choice and negotiation with oneself and those one lives with. It will remain a wellspring of diverse ideas in our field.

Developments in the political landscape affect everyone. We've all been moved by our increased proximity to war and conflict. We must continue to use our voice, even for humor. However, it may be that we will pursue our intensions more deliberately. Ceramists can celebrate and share their appreciation of connections among people.

What will the young ceramist of 2050 see in our work? There will be changes for sure. In 1929, Vally Wieselthier, a recent immigre from Vienna, wrote about her work. She felt that sculpture should be made with thrown sections added together to form what was in her case a human or animal figure. Her clay looked freshly put together. Wieselthier helped direct American sculpture away from the stiff Beaux Arts tradition to a pliant way of approaching form. Much of her work was later forgotten until a rethinking of figurative ceramic sculpture in the 1970s. Now it seems ludicrous that the fabrication process could be so rule-governed. Yet, seminal artists often do have a particular viewpoint and fortunately there is much diversity in these. If this thinking and rethinking continues, our field will remain healthy.

In contrast to the 20th century, it's been said that people in the 21st century will change careers/jobs 9 times on average. If this is true, it will certainly affect our field. Think of how many of our preeminent artists have devoted their entire lives to making fine pots and sculptures. Increasingly, artists may use clay for brief periods, or move from clay to multimedia or other media, perhaps making the role of the technical assistant increasingly important. Now workshops provide an easier way for people interested in ceramics to learn and have studio space. They offer an alternate form of education and inspiration. At least as early as the 1960s, academic ceramists began to give workshops in addition to their university teaching. Centers have sprouted, around the continent and around the world, modeled on the idea that a group of interested parties can build a workspace together, often led by masters of clay. This offers a blend of inspiration, performance and demonstration of very specific skills. There is a rapid pulse of energy at these centers. We need to know more about how this experience differs from traditional undergraduate or graduate programs.

I remain optimistic. There are still those fresh sublime breezes of "new" clay work and wake-up calls for us to pay attention to what life is about. Maybe there will come rallies for change or another lone stroke that will alter how we all look to our clay work. Exciting, cutting edge work is being done all over the world. North American work will, I think, be less likely to dominate globally as it did in the 1960s and 1970s. One agent of change will come from the thousands of immigrants as they participate in the North American cultural landscape. I count on them to make their roots and dreams visible.

Photos: Mark Eveson

Ann Mortimer

Newmarket, Ontario

"Quillions," 16.25 inches (41 cm) in height, slip-cast elements with low-fire glazes and quill inserts

"Tea Cock," 6.25 inches (16 cm) in height, low-fire slip-cast clay with slab addition and underglaze

Wayne Ngan

Hornby Island, British Columbia

"Male Vessel With Stone Base," 36 cm inches (91 cm) in height, thrown and sculpted stoneware

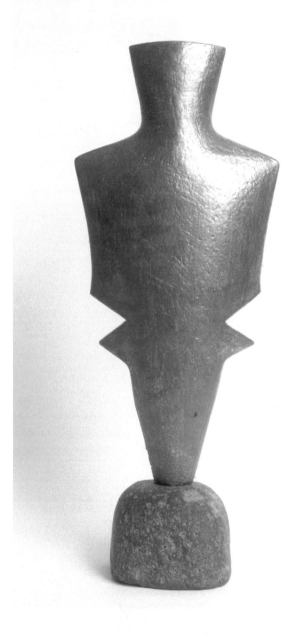

"Blue Abstract Vessel with Stacking Cup Base," 16 cm inches (41 cm) in height, salt-glazed stoneware

Photos: Robert Cain

Diane Nasr O'Young

Kleinburg, Ontario

"Basket," 15 inches (38 cm) in height, handbuilt, coiled and pinched porcelain, with sprayed glaze, fired to Cone 10-11 in reduction

"Basket," 25.5 inches (65 cm) in width, handbuilt, coiled and pinched porcelain, reduction-fired to Cone 10-11, sprayed with thin heavy-kaolin-based glaze

Photos: Yosh Inouye

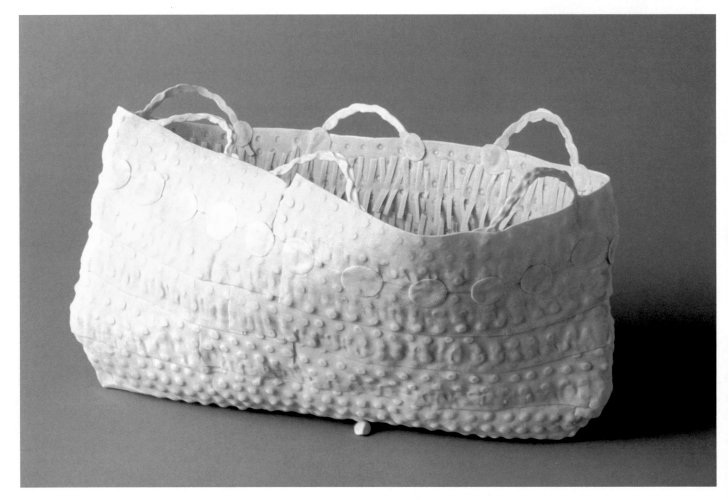

Kayo O'Young

Kleinburg, Ontario

Photos: Yosh Inouye

Jar with Insert of Smaller Piece Jar, 22.5 inches (57 cm) in height, wheel-thrown clay, with underglaze brushwork, reduction fired to Cone 10-11

Bowl, 11 inches (28 cm) in height, wheel-thrown porcelain, with underglaze brushwork, reduction fired to Cone 10-11

Matthias Ostermann

Montreal, Quebec

"Two Women," 14.5 inches (37 cm) in height, altered earthenware slab form with majolica white glaze and brushed stains, fired in oxidation

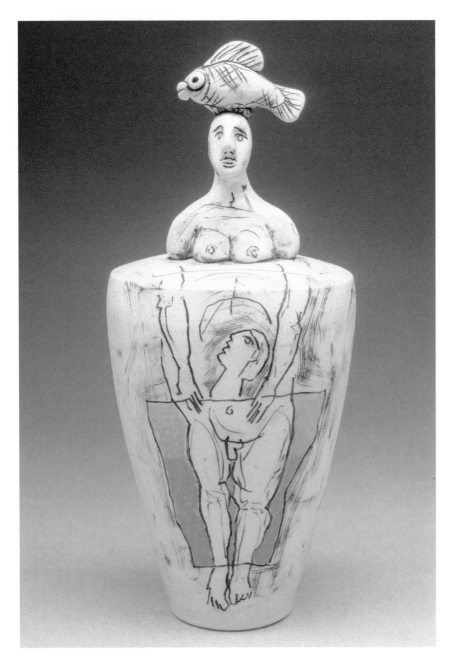

"Fisherman," 10.5 inches (27 cm) in height, thrown earthenware with sculpted lid, sgraffito, copper wash and vitreous slips, fired in oxidation

Walter Ostrom

Indian Harbour, Nova Scotia

"Dessert Plate, Botanical Drawing of Larch," 8.5 inches (22 cm) in width, press-molded earthenware with majolica glaze

"Dessert Plate, Botanical Drawing of Stamens and Pistols," 8.5 inches (22 cm) in width, press-molded earthenware with majolica glaze

"Blur," 16.5 inches (42 cm) in height, template-thrown earthenware with terra sigillatas, photo: Marc Hutchinson

"Tumblers," 5.5 inches (14 cm) in height, template-thrown earthenware with terra sigillatas, photo: Marc Hutchinson

Photo: Greg Payce

Pauline Pelletier

Cap Rouge, Quebec

Photos: Pierre Fortin

"Untitled," 12 inches (30 cm) in height, thrown earthenware, sawdust saggar fired to Cone 4 with soluble materials, gold leaf decoration after firing

"Untitled," 13 inches (33 cm) in height, cast earthenware, sawdust saggar fired to Cone 4 with soluble materials, gold leaf decoration after firing, intentionally broken and reconstructed

Kasia Piech

Hamilton, Ontario

"Small Rocking Horse," 9.5 inches (24 cm) in height, handbuilt, oxidation fired to Cone 3, with mixed media, glaze made from Shreddies, hot chocolate, lip gloss, baby powder, grape juice, frit and silicon carbide

Dolls, each 18 inches (46 cm) in height, handbuilt, oxidation fired to Cone 3, mixed media, glaze made from makeup, lipstick, eye shadow, blush, Rice Crispies, milk, orange juice, pudding, icing sugar, Mr. Freezes, a cherry drink, frit and silicon carbide

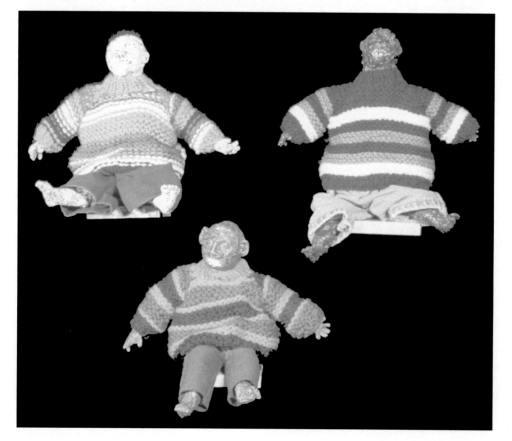

From the 20th to the 21st Century: A Woman in Ceramics

Ann Roberts

As the world moved shakily into the 21st century, I faced the task of cleaning my office of the leftovers from 27 years of teaching. What I found among the papers, photographs and books, was that more had changed in my life as an artist than the evolution of a body of work. A significant change was in attitude towards women by my colleagues, the art world, educational institutions and the world in general.

In the 1960s, the world of production potters was decidedly macho, with wall-to-wall stoneware production and catenary-arched, downdraft reduction kilns that produced oceans of iron-spotted ware. Innocently, I tottered into their world, making slip-glazed, and single-fired earthenware pots on a wheel in the kitchen of my Montreal apartment. I then trundled this work across town to fire at the Potters' Club. Somehow, along with women all over North America, I conquered glaze chemistry between cooking and diapering. As my pots became larger and more sculptural, it became necessary professionally to eliminate any mention of family life. It was fine for a man to be a professional potter and to have a family life, but for women, these conditions stamped you eternally as an amateur. The newspaper clippings I unearthed described how delightfully cute it was for a housewife to be potting as a hobby. Somewhere in each article, almost in passing, is the fact that my work was part of a national juried show or a solo exhibition. And always I was referred to by my husband's name, correctly prefaced by Mrs.

I found my copy of Bernard Leach's A *Potters Book* inscribed with the date and place I had acquired it: "1958 Cape Town, South Africa." What was it about that opening chapter "Towards a Standard" that drew me so strongly to his concept of the humble potter enthusiastically making repetitive production pottery for use in the kitchens of the world? How had I ever reconciled my varied basement studios with his Saint Ives Pottery? Canada in the 60s was awash in do-it-yourself crafts: weave your own cloth, make your own pots and roll your own.... It took a while before I noticed the discrepancies of Leach's life and writings. He was espousing the ethics of the male-dominated, Oriental folk artist to a Western society that was moving quickly toward a less-hierarchical arrangement.

The ceramic world of the 1970s was opening up in North America. Galleries found it useful to have a token ceramist and even a woman or two in their stable of artists. There was talk among ceramists of intellectual theories and college ceramics courses flourished. Many women whose postsecondary education had come adrift with motherhood went back to school. I joined them to study sculpture at a university where I learned primarily from male professors, and clay was considered only a means to an end. This meant casting it in bronze, cement or resin. I learned to keep a low profile to garner as much information as possible while continuing to work with fired clay at home. At my home university where I had taught part time, a fine arts department was evolving around courses taught by an enterprising woman who believed in a world of art undivided by media, gender or philosophical debate. I was energized by being surrounded by people who were positive in their acceptance of fired clay as an integral part of the sculpture program. As the faculty grew, the gender balance was kept consistently equal too. At last, being a woman in the late 70s became a liberating time. Who cared what the controversies and divisions were between potters and clay sculptors when there were goddesses to be discovered and feminist theories to be applied to the rationale for my frequently misconstrued images?

A visit in 1974-75 to the village potters of Lesotho had given me back my memories of the first 23 years of my life as a colonial child in Africa: stories only half remembered of the Earth Mother watching over shifting populations, eternal migrations, brave escapes and personal traumas. The rich heritage in myth and legend were no longer stale historical stories, but became again the concrete vestiges of the rites and rituals surrounding mortality and sexuality. Animals spoke and intervened in the lives of humans and the goddess was capable of holding the regenerative power of a springtime rebirth, or conversely, the seeds of death. I began to draw on threads of their stories and intertwine them with more recent travels to sacred places, stone circles and ancient burial sites.

Through the 1980s and 1990s I wove my own personal mythology from the experience of living on the banks of the Grand River. Rivers are most frequently considered to be female and in ancient mythology, fish were male, swimming in the River of Life. This opened up a series of life-sized female figures with fish. Women generally found the sculptures to be sensual and appealing while men were more often disturbed by the directness of the gaze and the women's casual nudity. One of the sculptures depicting a seated woman with half a fish in each hand is invariably viewed by even young males as a violent action. Can it be that they innately identify with the maleness of mythical fish?

For many years I made small maquettes before embarking on large-scale sculptures. I liked the physical sculptural presence of their volume and gesture as I worked on them in my studio. But in retrospect I probably did not work on a smaller scale for exhibitions in response to the male scorn bestowed upon ceramic sculpture as nick-knacks by a prominent art critic.

After visiting Greek museums and European "Venus" collections where the simplified human forms, some as old as 6000 years, generate a powerful hold on the viewer, I decided to similarly attempt to concentrate the gestures of humans and animals in a smaller scale.

My life as a woman now encompasses grandchildren. Viewing them endearingly interacting with pets, brought into sharp focus the animal power used in mythic legend to gain power and ascendancy through sexual dominance. It is a long stretch, but all narratives encompass the base desire for power. My boats may be a means of escape but the rabbits are symbols of survival and contain the essence of fertility and procreativity.

And that is surely what women will bring to the 21st century.

Peter Powning

Markhamville, New Brunswick

Photo: Beth Powning

"Horned Vase," 13.5 inches (34 cm) in height, thrown and altered, multi-fired clay, fired to Cone 04, photo: Peter Powning

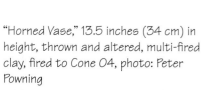

Fragmented Penumbrae," 15 inches (38 cm) in height, thrown and altered raku with cast bronze and copper, photo: Peter Powning

Ann Roberts

Conestogo, Ontario

"Anchored on Hades," 14.5 inches (37 cm) in height, handbuilt low-fire (Cone 02) white earthenware with alkaline glazes

"Adrift: Persephone 2003," 13.33 inches (34 cm) in height, handbuilt low-fire white earthenware with alkaline glazes

Laurie Rolland

Sechelt, British Columbia

Photo: Larry Westlake

"Didymous Series #8, 2003,"
15 inches (38 cm) in height,
handbuilt using a wooden push-
through mold, oxide wash and
sprayed glaze, fired to Cone 6
in an electric kiln, photo: Laurie
Rolland

"Circinate Series #3, 2003,"
7 inches (18 cm) in height,
handbuilt using a wooden push-
through mold, sprayed interior
glaze, brushed oxide and slip-
washed exterior, fired to Cone 6
in an electric kiln, photo: Laurie
Rolland

Maurice Savoie

Longueuil, Quebec

"Metamorphose II 2001," 18 inches (46 cm)
in height, porcelain with fractured structure,
partially glazed, with metal, photo: Pierre Gauvin

Metamorphose V 2003, 19 inches (48 cm)
in height, porcelain with fractured structure,
partially glazed, photo: Pierre Gauvin

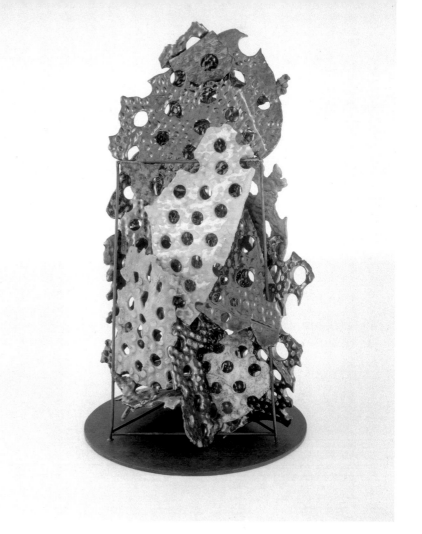

Tom Smith

Saint Andrews, New Brunswick

"Torn Rim Vessel," 9 inches (23 cm) in height, raku fired with soda ash in a glaze containing copper and cobalt carbonates

"Torn Rim Vessel," 10 inches (25 cm) in height, raku fired with red and white terra sigillata and a splash of salt with copper sulfate

Jack Sures

Regina, Saskatchewan

"Balancing Act,"
14 inches (36 cm)
in height, thrown
porcelain with cobalt
oxide

"Bowl of Fruit; Plate,"
20 inches (51 cm)
in diameter, thrown
porcelain with brushed
cobalt oxide over
celadon glaze

R. Jan Symons

Toronto, Ontario

Flower Brick, 8.5 inches (22 cm) in width, handbuilt red earthenware with polychrome glazes

"Squid Tail Nung Dish," 16 inches (41 cm) in width, handbuilt red earthenware with sgrafitto and polychrome glazes

Across the Digital Divide with a Fistful of Mud

"Can I make a living as an artist?"

John Glick

I recall vividly the excitement we graduate ceramics students felt in 1961 when we were given the chance to unpack and install The Syracuse National, a pottery exhibition that visited Cranbrook Academy of Art on tour. What I remember keenly was the excitement of opening crates and unwrapping pots by well-known potters of that time. I recall that a casserole by Ken Ferguson had special meaning for me. It's rich glaze and inspired simplicity of form invited touch. Yes, we actually got to touch the pots. Amazing!

This touches, so strongly for me, something deeper about our potter's lore. It is about the concept of touch and being in touch. We potters are rightly in love with touch. And we now stay in touch with our field in additional and very different ways (email, transmitting images, websites and other means) along with the familiar ways I have described in my student-time memories. To some degree I refer to my own love affair with digital media although I admit to being in an ongoing love/struggle with the digital world.

Still, this is about something so basic and so familiar that it bears restating every so often. What was so moving for us as we reverently held those inspired pots of the 1960s had to do

with how we learn and grow as artists. It was about influence and enrichment and being stretched and required to look beyond our own horizons.

Now another generation of potters will look at this marvelous collection of clay art that is titled, "21st Century Ceramics in the United States and Canada," and amazingly, the time between 1961 and 2003 will shrink down to what feels like mere days...weeks at best. So, what has changed? Everything and nothing.

I came away from that exposure to the potters of that earlier time filled with respect and excitement. I suspect many will feel similar feelings about this present exhibit and book. The key is that the power to move and awe and inspire is still as potent as ever.

I also know that there are deeply-felt concerns about the clay field's viability in this bewilderingly complex world we share. Somehow having crossed the digital divide has also upped the ante. Increasingly the question, "Can I make a living as an artist?" seems to carry with it even greater complexity and apprehension.

Not surprisingly, this is the question that comes up each year in my own studio as I talk with my studio assistant about his/her future plans. "Can I make it as an artist in today's world?" was my own very concern-laden question from those many years ago...now

still the very real concern for today.

So, how to navigate in this post-digital world is the key question. And, the answer is the *same* as it always was... it is about connecting!

Staying passionate about what matters to you in your work is a beginning. Being unable to stop making what you believe in and continuing to make the work that gets you up in the morning and burns in your gut long after the sun goes down is the rock on which to build. It means listening to instinctive signals coming from your soul that tell you about the path to follow.

This is what the artists I know have done over the length of long careers. They have continued their commitment to their work with passion and continued to ask the kinds of questions that propel the work forward.

And, if the work you make nourishes your spirit, there is a chance that it can reach others. Something has to be there to feel and if you put it there, then it is accessible for others. This is what has made it possible for generations of artists to feel heard and understood over the din of life around them.

So, sitting there with my studio assistant, mugs of tea in hand, our feet propped up and doing what we love to do from time to time... talking deeply about what matters. After much is pondered, I say, "Absolutely! You can do it. Nothing has changed."

Bruce Taylor

Waterloo, Ontario

"Untitled (Black Cone)," 32 inches (81 cm) in height, ceramics with terra sigillata and copper leaf

"Untitled (Copper Capsule)," 20 inches (51 cm) in height, ceramics with terra sigillata and copper leaf

Jim Thomson

Ottawa, Ontario

"Inverted Shoebridge," 12 inches (30 cm) in height, handbuilt clay with underglaze and ash glaze, fired to Cone 6 in oxidation

"I Saw the Lucierie Thing (Purple)," 20 inches (51 cm) in height, handbuilt and thrown clay with underglaze and glaze, fired to Cone 6 in oxidation

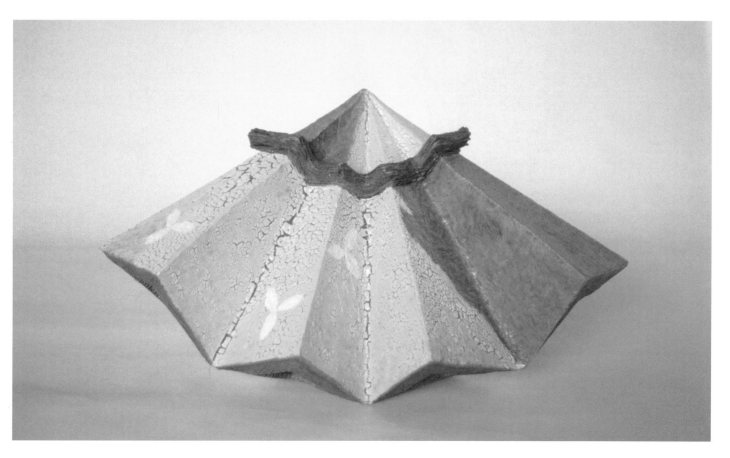

Barbara Tipton

Calgary, Alberta

"Barque," 9.5 inches (24 cm) in height, handbuilt paper clay with low-fire slips and glazes, multifired, photo: Barbara Tipton

"Orange Torso," 11 inches (28 cm) in height, handbuilt paper clay with low-fire slips, glazes and computer-generated laser decals, photo: Barbara Tipton

Ghost Handles

John Chalke

Designed to raise a frown and eventually soft hackles, the hoary "Where Do We Go from Here?" can be a colorless question probably only asked by conference organizers, non-makers, thesis specialists and lost rally drivers. I personally don't know of any potter/clay artist who particularly dwells on such heady stuff. Why? For now we go on to the next firing. That's where I'd like to go. Did the questioner mean access to materials, better fuel costs, availability of the Muse?

I find myself dealing more with: Where did I just come from? Meaning, what was the origin of the work I made a little while ago. In this light, parts of the two pitchers I sent to "21st Century Ceramics..." originate from around the end of the 19th century in the Jutland area of Denmark. Hazy recollections, however, seeing as the seed sowed itself well over 35 years ago. But I hold to two connections—one slightly less in focus than another. The first: two Danish potters who came to work one summer in a rural pottery near where I was living in

England. They made handles conventionally, and then less so. The less so was to tease the handle—tubular...out of the parent thrown form and kind of squeeze it into a lifting device of trust and certainty. I thought it clever, even wondrous, but left it alone. It was their affair for now, these two women with their unusual sandwiches and strange exclamations in the semi-gloom of the drying floor.

The other connection was a poorly printed black-and-white photograph from a library. (Alas, where? For I have been to many libraries.) An image of a Jutland farmhouse kitchen, with a sturdy wooden table, a mixing bowl, and this pitcher, this jug, with an odd handle. Surely, here was that handle. I looked at it through a large magnifying glass for more enlightenment but merely got flung a face full of halftone dots.

About seven years ago I determined to find one of the Danish potters, to ask her about that handle she knew. Wonderfully, I found that she was still around, now living by herself in a quiet house with a high-walled garden where we had afternoon tea. Ah, no, she didn't remember the handle. Don't remember? But you must....

Common Ground World Project

Bill Hunt

It's hard to imagine a ceramic work more 21st century, or what we hope for 21st century ceramics than Neil Tetkowski's "Common Ground World Project." Tetkowski, with the help of a few thousand others, collected a kilo of clay (or in the case of nations without clay, sand) from each of the 188 member states in the United Nations. It was a unifying experience as he traveled, corresponded with, talked to and faxed clay-gatherers around the world. He then combined these samples into a single clay body from which he formed at the U.N. a large mandala. Into this wet clay form, he directed a citizen of each nation to place a small tablet of their individual nation's clay, which he had prepared for them. These tablets were placed to form a large spiral emanating from two handprints, one inside the other. The larger one was from a 100-year-old woman, representing the start of the last millennium. The smaller print was from the hand of a baby born the first day of the 21st century. Thus, the mandala visually states the interconnection of all people of all ages from all nations.

All the ceremony and most of the making took place inside the visitor's entrance to the U.N. During this time of incompleteness, Tetkowski had previously produced drawings of what was to come and a piece composed of bottles, each containing the clay of a different nation. The exhibition "Common Ground World Project" has been traveling to museums since it's inception and was shown in conjunction with "21st Century Ceramics in the United States and Canada."

LEFT: Neil Tetkowski's mandala, the centerpiece of the "Common Ground World Project" was displayed at the United Nations Building in New York City.

TOP: Tetkowski with the leather-hard mandala in his temporary studio at the U.N. The piece was made from clay or sand from each U.N.-represented nation, combined into one clay body.

ABOVE AND RIGHT (DETAIL): Bottles containing clay or sand from each of the 188 member states are arranged on an aluminum table as a sculptural artform.

Valuations of Contemporary Ceramics

*Valuations listed here are the values given to the organizers of
the 21st Century Ceramics exhibition for purposes of sales or as an
insurance value in the case of works not for sale.*

UNITED STATES

Dean Adams 2
"Holes"
US$1600
"Slots"
US$1600

Richard Aerni 3
"Gondola Tray"
US$100
Bowl
US$300

Stanley Mace Andersen 4
Coffee Server
US$200
Tureen and Plate
US$300

Dan Anderson 5
"Shell Water Tower"
US$3000
"Gulf Water Tower"
US$3000

Frederica Antonio 6
NA

Linda Arbuckle 7
"Square Bowl: Twos on Red"
US$250
"Oval: Toward Fall"
US$225

Adrian Arleo 8
"Land & Sky"
US$3200
"Woman with Reclined
    Blue Child"
US$3000

Rudy Autio 9
"Memorial"
US$75000

Clayton Bailey 10
"Urn for the Unconceived"
US$2000

Doug Baldwin 11
"Large Tray with Ducks"
US$1800
"Small Ball Game"
US$800

John Balistreri 12
"Wing-Map"
US$7000
"Jet"
US$3000

Mary Barringer 13
Platter With Handhold
US$475
Basin With Ears
US$425

Bennett Bean 14
"Triple on Base Master #803"
US$22000
"Pair on Base Master #1000"
US$8000

Peter Beasecker 15
Carrier
US$1250
Ewer
US$650

Susan Beiner 16
"Hidden Agenda: Hair-Do #2"
US$1800
"New Hybrids"
US$350

Joe Bennion 17
Faceted Tea Bowl
US$50
Pitcher
US$75

Curt Benzle 18
"Life Flutters By"
US$950
"Break on Through"
US$1750

Rick Berman 19
"Salku Bottle"
US$1500
"Salku Vase"
US$1500

Luis Bermudez 20
"El Caracol"
US$4800
"Las tre Culebras"
US$6000

Gina Bobrowski 21
"Swan"
US$3000

Mary Jo Bole 22
"Granny's Necklace (A Bench)"
US$15000
"Plaque"
US$750

Joe Bova 23
"Rabbit Canopic"
US$800
"Red Monkey Jar"
US$800

Frank Boyden 24
"Speaking with Herons"
US$7500
"2 Owl Vase"
US$2000

Bruce Breckenridge 25
"Huntington Park #18"
US$4000
"Huntington park #19"
US$6000

Richard Bresnehan 26
Jar
US$9000
Teapot
US$1200

Cynthia Bringle 27
Set of 6 Goblets
US$900
"Vessel with Turtle & Fish"
US$2800

William C. Brouillard 30
"Killer Bees"
US$245
"The Tin Man's Whiskey Bottle"
US$210

Barbara Brown 31
Zen Plate Series: "Earth"
US$250
Vase Form
US$120

Susan Budge 32
"Crown"
US$4500
"Ra"
US$4500

Vincent P. Burke 33
"On Prufrock and other
    Observations #5"
US$1200
"Regarding Grace"
US$3000

Richard Burkett 34
"Pressure Vessel: Teatime
    for Big Oil"
US$800
"Pressure Vessel: Overregulated"
US$800

Bill Campbell 35
"Falling Water"
US$510
"Sail On"
US$510

Virginia Cartwright 36
"Folded Teapot with
    Inlaid Cobalt Porcelain"
US$275
Teapot Set
US$435

Doug Casebeer 37
Vase
US$150 each
Pitcher
US$150

Marek Cecula 38
"Servings #6"
US$3000
"Servings #4"
US$3000

Aurore Chabot 39
"Malaprop"
US$2500
"Fungus Map"
US$2000

Paul Chaleff 40
Jar Form
US$5000
Three-Part Form
US$4000

Linda Christianson 41
Cooking Oil Can
US$250
Two Striped Plates
US$75

Sam Chung 42
"Teapot (green/black)"
US$400
"Teapot (black/blue dots)"
US$400

Elaine Coleman 44
Bowl
US$1400
Covered Jar
US$2000

Tom Coleman 45
White Stoneware Ikebana
US$1200
Vase
US$2000

Scott Cooper 46
Fluted Celadon Vase
US$100
Carbon Trap Shino Bowl
US$60

Kevin Crowe 47
Thrown and Paddled Vase
US$1200
Altered vase
US$350

Anne Currier 48
"Zoar"
US$10000
"Pivotal Moment 2002"
US$8000

Val Cushing 49
"Covered Jar/Column Series"
US$2000
"Covered Jar/Column Series"
US$2000

Kathy Dambach 50
"Toy Series...Bobber"
US$5000
"Toy Series...Over & Over
    & Over & Over"
US$8000

Malcom Davis 51
Personal Teapot
US$500
Shino Teabowl
US$500

Harris Deller 52
"Untitled Wall Platter
    with Concentric Arcs"
US$2500
"Untitled Wall Platter
    with Ellipse #2"
US$1500

Josh DeWeese 53
Jar
US$150
Pitcher
US$150

Kim Dickey 54
"Tart Bush"
US$8000
"Beauty Bush"
US$8000

Barbara Diduk 55
"Max and Moritz"
US$2000
"Yellow & Black Still Life"
US$200

Marylyn Dintenfass 58
"Nerige Column"
US$8500
"Nerige Horizon"
US$6500

Gary DiPasquale 59
Tall Vase
US$1600
Double Neck Vase
US$650

Eddie Dominguez 60
"Red Twister"
US$4500
"Road through the Storm"
US$4500

Paul Dresang 61
"Bag"
US$5000
"Photo Op"
US$3600

Ed Eberle 62
"Black Field"
US$12000

Kim Ellington 63
Six Gallon Jar
US$600
Two Gallon Jar
US$325

Seo Eo 64
"Vapor"
NA (Installation)

Paul Eshelman 65
"Round and Square
    Shoulder Vase"
US$100
"Bump Bowls"
US$270

Cary Esser 66
"Sarracenia"
US$2800
"Ploughed Under"
US$2600

Christine Federighi 67
"'Wrapped and Protected'
    Dog"
US$4000
"'Wrapped and Protected'
    Dog Guide"
US$4000

Ken Ferguson 68
"White Bull On Cart"
US$5000
"Charging Bull on Platter"
US$5000

Anita Fields 69
"Evidence Seen"
US$7000
"Reaching #1"
US$4600

Susan Filley 70
"Regal Teapot - Starry Blue"
US$750
"Tray - Tango Twist"
US$250

Angela Fina 71
Fan-Shaped Container for
    Flower Arranging
US$190
Set of Five Flower Containers
US$230

Verne Funk 72
"Painted Head"
US$8600
"Head On"
US$6200

David Furman 73
"Mama Mumbo / Tin Can
    TPot, 2003"
US$2500
"Little Guy / Tin Can TPot"
US$1900

John Glick 74
Plate
US$3500
"Landscape View Sculpture"
US$3000

DeBorah Goletz 75
Stacked Serving Set
    with Bud Vase
US$800
Stacked Serving Bowls
    with Bud Vase
US$500

John Goodheart 76
"Skill and Reason"
US$3000
"End of Search"
US$3000

Jane Graber 79
"Americana Dreams I"
US$1500
"Americana Dreams II"
US$900

Juan Granados 80
"Germination"
US$3000
"Support"
US$3000

Bill Griffith 81
"Dwelling #1"
US$1100
"Dwelling #2"
US$900

Chris Gustin 82
Vase
US$7500
Bowl
US$4000

Susan Harris 83
"Zhong with Bufonidae"
US$1200
"Flask with Armadillo"
US$800

Robert Harrison 84
"Tapering Rectangular
    Clay Window"
US$500
"Lotus-Arch Clay Window"
US$450

Rebecca Harvey 85
"Marco/Polo"
US$800
"Duck Stack"
US$750

Gwen Heffner 86
"Triplets"
US$600
"Gold Urchin Teapot"
US$300

Tony Hepburn 87
"www.rack, 2000"
US$6000
"Revolution"
US$7000

Mark Hewitt 88
"The Sultan's Two Lips
    (Large Vase)"
US$5000
"Requiem Grave Marker"
US$5000

Catharine Hiersoux 89
Wood-Fired Vase
US$1200
Wood-Fired Vase
US$950

Wayne Higby 90
"Green River Gorge"
US$6000
"Fidolon Creek"
US$6000

Steven Hill 91
Melon Pitcher
US$380
Bowl
US$340

Chuck Hindes 92
Wood-Fired Jar
US$600
Wood-Fired Tea Bowl
US$600

Anne E. Hirondelle 93
"Outurn 28"
US$2250
"Outurn 31"
US$2250

Rick Hirsch 94
Alter Bowl #35
US$3500
Mortar and Pestle #4
US$3500

Thomas Hoadley 95
"Untitled (#616)"
US$2025
"Untitled (#666)"
US$3150

Curtis Hoard 96
"Vase with Dog Figures"
NA
"Vase with Bird and Figures"
NA

Patrick Horsley 97
"T-pot/Purple"
US$1000
"Boat Vase"
US$170

Cary Hulin 98
Teapot
US$80
Small Storage Jar
US$65

Sylvia Hyman 99
"Crate of Books and Things"
US$5400
"Tomato Box with Blueprints"
US$6000

Sarah Jaeger 100
Tureen and Tray
US$400
Bowl
US$350

Randy Johnston 101
"Boat Form"
US$2000
Vase Form
US$2000

Louis Katz 102
"Recumbent Batter Bowl"
US$460
"Recumbent Bowl"
US$460

Diane Kenney 103
Covered Jar
US$250
Serving Bowl
US$200

Tom Kerrigan 104
"Desert Flora XXII"
US$2200
"Desert Flora XV"
US$2000

Y.C. Kim 105
"Ice and Water Series: 0303"
US$2000
"Melting Away: 0208"
US$1200

Peter King & Xinia Marin 106
"Templo De Martes, 2001"
US$125000
"The Great Experiment 2001,
    911 Homage to America"
US$125000